Introduction

Offensive defense systems are one of the basic elements of youth handball – through creation of large spaces in width and depth, they promote the individual players' development both as offense and defense players. In the first place, offensive man coverage should be practiced. Through clear, fixed coverage of their respective opponent, the defense players have a well-defined responsibility which may result in the development of their individual defense play. In small groups, the players practice how to interact with and support each other step by step before they learn how to play the first variants of a two-line zone defense (1-5 and 3-3 defense systems).

The exercises in this collection teach the basics of offensive defense play, with defending against the player in ball possession both by stealing the ball and 1-on-1, defending against players without a ball and shielding off the pivot, moving along with the opponent, and anticipatory defense play with interrupting passes and stealing the ball.

The second part of the collection deals with cooperation in small groups in order to defend against positional changes of the attacking players in the width and with a two-line defense play against back players and the pivot(s).

The last exercises consist of a drill series dealing with offensive man coverage and moving back to ball level as well as 1-5 and 3-3 defense systems before finally a more defensive, 3-2-1 defense system is introduced.

Publishing information

1 st English edition released on 06 Jan 2019
German original edition released on 26 Nov 2018

Published by DV Concept
Editors, design, and layout: Jörg Madinger, Elke Lackner
Proofreading and English translation: Nina-Maria Nahlenz

ISBN: 978-3-95641-238-7

This publication is listed in the catalogue of the **German National Library**. Please refer to http://dnb.de for bibliographic data.

The work and its components are protected by copyright. No reprinting, photomechanical reproduction, storing or processing in electronic systems without the publisher's written permission.

Training of offensive defense systems in youth handball
1-on-1, small groups, man coverage, and offensive defense cooperation

Contents:

No.	Name	Players	Difficulty level	Page
Category: Individual basics				
1. Preparatory games and exercises				
1	Tag rally	6	★	6
2	Tag game with a queue	5	★	7
3	Tiger ball	7	★	8
4	4-on-4 tag game	10	★	9
5	Preparatory exercise with bibs	2	★	10
6	Defense movements with tennis ball and handball	2	★	11
2. Stealing the ball 1-on-1				
7	Stealing the ball after observing the opponent	2	★	12
8	Ball stealing variants	2	★	14
9	Stealing the ball in a predefined corridor	2	★	15
10	Stealing the ball with varying attacking players	8	★	16
11	Stealing the ball and shooting at the goal	9	★	17
12	Stealing the ball 1-on-1 on command	3	★★	18
3. Offensive 1-on-1 defense				
13	1-on-1 for three players	3	★	19
14	Preventing passes	3	★	20
15	Preventing a breakthrough with and without a ball	8	★	21
16	1-on-1 game on mats	8	★	22
17	Three times 1-on-1 in a corridor	10	★	23
18	Two times 1-on-1 in a corridor	9	★	24
19a	1-on-1 with simultaneous observing of the player in ball possession	9	★★	25
19b	1-on-1 with simultaneous observing of the player in ball possession	9	★★	26
20	1-on-1 with offensive defense lines – Moving back and attacking subsequently	7	★★★	27
4. Catching and stealing the ball				
21	Series of shots with catching and stealing the ball	6	★	28
22	Series of shots with catching and stealing the ball 2	8	★	29
23a	Catching and stealing the ball from the defense position – Basic exercise	7	★	30
23b	Catching and stealing the ball from the defense position – Advanced exercise	7	★	31
24	Catching and stealing the ball following 1-on-1 actions	9	★★	32
25	Catching and stealing the ball from the wing positions	8	★★	33
5. Defense against the pivot in offensive defense systems				
26	Shielding off the pivot to prevent passes	7	★	34
27	Shielding off the pivot to prevent passes 2	4	★	35
28	Shielding off the pivot to prevent passes 3	7	★	36

Training of offensive defense systems in youth handball
1-on-1, small groups, man coverage, and offensive defense cooperation

No.	Name	Players	Difficulty level	Page
6. Defense against the second pivot in offensive defense systems				
29	Moving along with the second pivot	7	★	37
30	Moving along with the second pivot and playing 2-on-2	9	★	38
31a	Moving along with the second pivot from the wing position	7	★	39
31b	Moving along with the second pivot from the wing position and preventing a breakthrough	7	★★	40
32	Moving along with the second pivot from the back positions and defending against two pivots	9	★★	41
Category: Small group defense				
1. Cooperation across the width of the defense zone				
33	2-on-2 competition	8	★	42
34	2-on-2 defense in a corridor and supporting each other in case of a breakthrough	9	★	43
35	2-on-2 defense in a corridor with handing/taking over in case of crossing movements	10	★★	44
36	2-on-2 defense in a corridor with and without a ball against crossing moves and overlapping	10	★★	45
37	2-on-2 switch game	12 (14)	★★	47
38	3-on-3 defense	6	★★	48
2. Cooperation throughout the depth of the defense zone				
39	Shielding off two pivots to prevent passes from the back positions	10	★	49
40	2-on-2 against a back position player and a pivot	7	★	50
41	3-on-3 against two back position players and the pivot	9	★	52
42	Defending against the back position players and the pivot 4-on-4	9	★	54
43a	Shielding off and communicating: Pivot standing at the 6-meter line	7	★★	55
43b	Shielding off and communicating: Pivot standing offensively between the 7- and 9-meter lines	7	★★	57
43c	Shielding off and communicating: Pivot standing on the ball side	7	★★	58
43d	Shielding off and communicating: Pivot standing on the non-ball side	7	★★	59
43e	Shielding off and communicating: Pivot making a screening attempt	7	★★	60
Category: Team defense and offensive defense cooperation				
1. Offensive man coverage with moving back to ball level				
44	Supporting each other in case of a breakthrough 3-on-3	7	★	61
45	Defending and moving back to ball level	9	★	62
46	3-on-3 and man coverage with moving back to ball level	7	★	63
47	5-on-5 man coverage with moving back to ball level	11	★	64
48	6-on-6 man coverage with moving back to ball level	13	★	65

No.	Name	Players	Difficulty level	Page
2. Defending in a 1-5 defense system				
49	1-on-1 and defending against the pivot in a 1-5 defense system	10	★★	66
50	1-5 defense system: Small groups of back and wing players with catching/stealing the ball on the center back position	10	★★	67
51a	1-5 defense system 4-on-4	9	★★	68
51b	1-5 defense system 6-on-6	13	★★	70
52a	Defending against a second pivot from the wing position	12	★★	71
52b	Defending against a second pivot from the back position by moving along and handing over	9	★★	72
52c	1-5 defense system 6-on-6	13	★★	73
3. Defending in a 3-3 defense system				
53	3-on-3 defense in a corridor against positional changes of the attacking players	10	★★	74
54	3-3 defense system: Foremost defense line against crossing moves and second pivot	10	★★	75
55	3-3 defense system: Defending on the wing and center back positions	11	★★	76
56	3-3 defense system 6-on-6	13	★★	78
4. Defending in a 3-2-1 defense system				
57	Preparatory 1-on-1 exercise and moving back to the pivot	10	★★★	79
58	4-on-4 defense diamond	8	★★★	80
59	Offensive defense wing player on the opposite side in a 3-2-1 defense system	8	★★★	81
60	3-2-1 defense system 6-on-6	13	★★★	83

Editor's note

Further reference books published by DV Concept

Training of offensive defense systems in youth handball
1-on-1, small groups, man coverage, and offensive defense cooperation

Key:

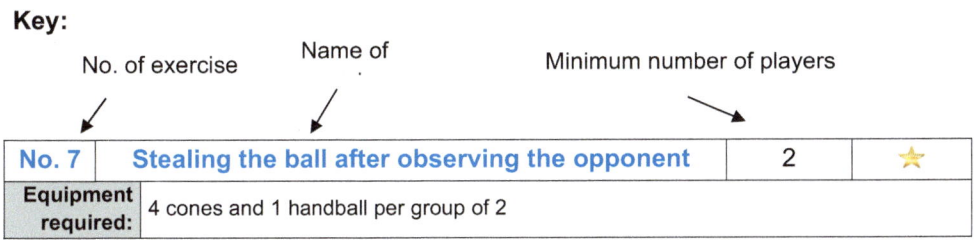

No. 7	**Stealing the ball after observing the opponent**	2	★
Equipment required:	4 cones and 1 handball per group of 2		

✗	Cone
⬛	Ball box
☐	Small vaulting box (upside down)
▬ ▬	Small gym mat
▬▬▬	Balance bench
⊥	Pole
🟠🟡🟪	Bib
▬▬▬	Foam noodles (foam beams)
●	Tennis ball

The exercises are divided into the following difficulty levels:

★   This exercise can be done both by beginners and well-advanced players and is intended to develop basic defense skills.

★★   This exercise requires some experience but may be done by players of all age groups with appropriate adaptation.

★★★   This exercise is more complex and requires proficiency in the basic skills.

Training of offensive defense systems in youth handball
1-on-1, small groups, man coverage, and offensive defense cooperation

Category: Individual basics

1. Preparatory games and exercises

No. 1	Tag rally	6	★
Equipment required:	6 cones		

Setting:
- Define two playing fields of suitable size with cones.
- The players spread out on the two playing fields, as shown in the example with six players per field.

Course:
- ①, ②, ③, and ④ lie down on the floor face down and towards the center, as shown in the figure.
- ② is the catcher (B).
- ① takes quick turns and tries to avoid being caught (A).
- If ① jumps over a player, who is lying on the floor (e.g. ①) (C), this player becomes the new catcher and must try to catch ② (D). ① lies down on the floor in the former position of ①.
- If a catcher (②) manages to catch the fleeing player (①) before he has jumped over another player, the players switch roles and the former fleeing player becomes the catcher.
- The group in the other field does the same course.

⚠ The groups should not be too large, otherwise the players will have to wait for too long until it is their turn.

⚠ Request immediate adjusting to the lying, catching, and fleeing situations (short reaction time, permanent change of tasks).

Training of offensive defense systems in youth handball
1-on-1, small groups, man coverage, and offensive defense cooperation

No. 2	Tag game with a queue	5	★
Equipment required:			

Setting:
- Make groups of 4 to 6 players each.

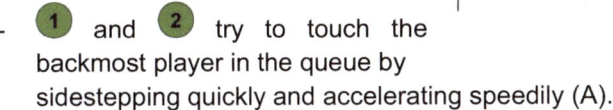

Course:
- All the players of each group line up and hold each other by their hips.
- One player per group does not join the line (① and ② in the figure) but stands in front of the first player in the queue (▲1 and ▲5 in the figure).
- ① and ② try to touch the backmost player in the queue by sidestepping quickly and accelerating speedily (A).
- ▲1 and ▲5 try to prevent this for as long as they can by obstructing the way (B) and closing the gap between ①/② and the queue.
- The group also may move away from the attacking player (C). While doing this, the players must not let go of each other but always maintain their queue.
- As soon as the coach whistles, ▲1 and ▲5 leave the group and try to touch the last player in the group during the next round; ①/② take over the positions at the end of the respective queue.
- Repeat until each player has caught one time.

⚠ ▲1 and ▲5 should always try to obstruct the way to the backmost player by doing quick steps and intensive leg work.

⚠ The catchers should work actively, take turns and change their speed over and over.

⚠ The longer the queue, the easier the catchers' task and the more demanding is the task for the first players in the queue.

No. 3	Tiger ball	7	★
Equipment required:	1 handball		

Course:
- Five players sit on the floor in a circle and keep passing a ball (A).
- ① and ② try to catch and steal the ball through intensive legwork.
- If they manage to catch and steal the ball (B), or if the ball gets lost, the player who played the last pass switches tasks with the defense player who has been playing defense longest at that time.

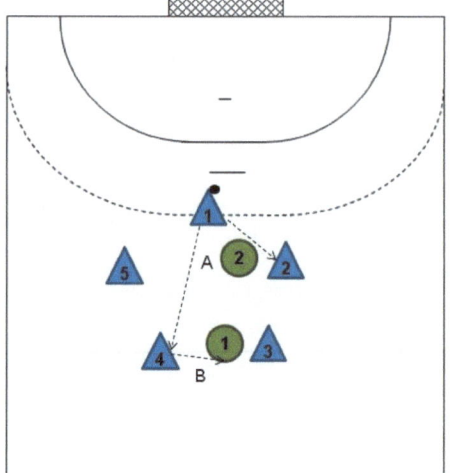

⚠ The attacking players should pass the ball quickly. Additional rule (if applicable). If a player holds the ball for more than three seconds, he has to switch tasks with the defense player.

⚠ The defense players should work together and force the passing players to make mistakes through active movement and feints.

⚠ The ball must not be kicked out.

Variants:
- The players do not sit but stand (on one foot). In this case, the players are not allowed to play banana passes.

Training of offensive defense systems in youth handball
1-on-1, small groups, man coverage, and offensive defense cooperation

No. 4	4-on-4 tag game	10	★
Equipment required:	6 cones, 1 handball		

Setting:
- Define a field with cones (or existing lines on the gym floor).
- Four defense players stand in the field.

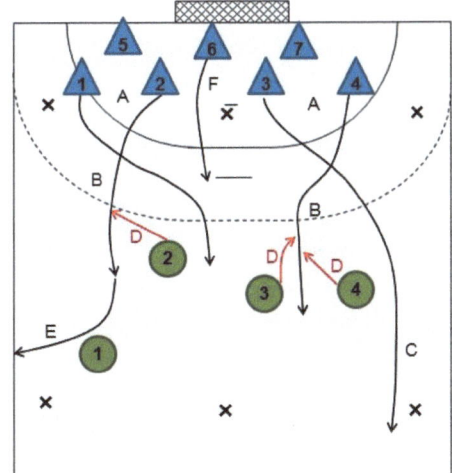

Course:
- Four attacking players (1, 2, 3, and 4) start simultaneously (A) and try to cross the field and the backmost line (B and C). The defense players (1, 2, 3, and 4) try to tag the running players (D).
- While doing this, the attacking players may work together, i.e. one attacking player may bind two defense players (B) so that another attacking player is able to cross the field (C).
- If an attacking player has been tagged, he must leave the field via the side lines (E).
- As soon as a player has left the field (C and E), a new player may start (F).
- Attacking players who left the field line up again.
- The offense team gets a point for each attacking player who has crossed the backmost line; the defense team gets a point for each tagged attacking player.
- Change the defense players after several actions. The winner on points (offense or defense) may choose an extra task for the losing team (e.g. sit-ups, turning cartwheels, push-ups).

⚠ Only four attacking players may be in the field at a time. However, the attacking players should start with a new player immediately once a teammate has left the field in order to put the defense players under maximum pressure (through four active opponents).

⚠ The attacking players should collaborate, cross, and distract so that a teammate can cross the field uninterruptedly.

⚠ The defense players should move actively and communicate with each other.

Training of offensive defense systems in youth handball
1-on-1, small groups, man coverage, and offensive defense cooperation

No. 5	Preparatory exercise with bibs	2	★
Equipment required:	2 bibs of different color per group of 2		

Setting 1:
- Two players stand face-to-face.
- One player holds a colored bib in each hand (the bibs have different colors, e.g. yellow and green).

Course 1:
- As soon as the coach whistles, the player with the bibs drops one of them. If he drops the bib in his right hand, the other player must catch it with his left (opposite) hand, before it touches the ground. If he drops the left bib, the other player must catch it with his right (opposite) hand, before it touches the ground.

⚠ Younger players may throw the bib in the air a bit instead of just dropping it, so that there is more time to think about which hand should be used.

Setting 2:
- 🔺 and ① now stand face-to-face at a larger distance to each other (approx. 2 meters).
- 🔺 holds a colored bib in each hand (different colors, e.g. yellow and green).
- As soon as the coach whistles, 🔺 drops one of the bibs (A).
- ① should do 1-2 quick steps forward and catch the bib, before it touches the ground (B).
- If 🔺 drops the yellow bib, ① must catch it with his right hand, before it touches the ground. If 🔺 drops the green bib, ① must catch it with his left hand, before it touches the ground.

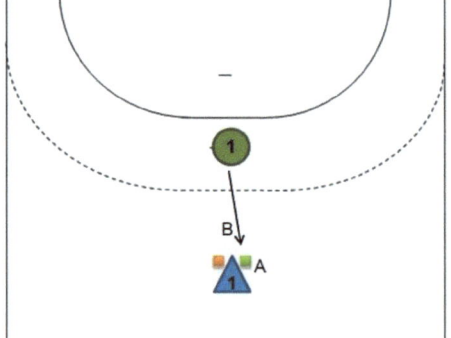

Variants:
- If the coach whistles twice, the player should change the catching hand.
- 🔺 holds a handball in each hand. As soon as the coach whistles, he drops one of them. ① should now catch the ball according to the same rules and before it bounces on the floor (bounces a second time).

| No. 6 | Defense movements with tennis ball and handball | 2 | ★ |

Equipment required: One tennis ball and one handball per team of 2

Setting:
- The teams make groups of 2.
- Each group has a tennis ball and a handball.

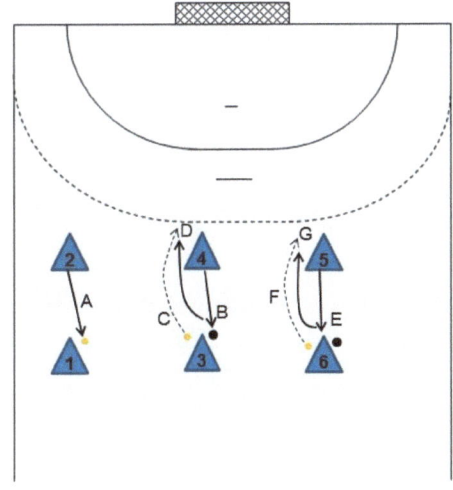

Course 1 (A):
- ① and ② stand face-to-face at a distance of about 2-3 meters; ① has a tennis ball.
- ① bounces the tennis ball on the floor.
- ② sprints forward and tries to catch the tennis ball before it bounces on the floor a second time (A).
- Afterwards, ② bounces the ball, and so on, until each player has done five sprints.
- If the players are able to catch the ball, they increase the distance during the next round; if they were not able to catch the ball, they may shorten the distance.

Course 2 (B to D):
- ③ and ④ stand face-to-face at a distance of about 2-3 meters; ③ has a tennis ball and a handball.
- ③ starts bouncing the handball.
- ④ sprints forward and tries to steal the ball (dribbling) (B).
- After stealing the ball, ③ easily throws the tennis ball over ④ (C) as if he would play a banana pass.
- ④ turns around and tries to catch the tennis ball while it is in the air (D).
- After five actions each, the players switch tasks.

Course 3 (E to G):

- 5 and 6 stand face-to-face at a distance of about 2-3 meters; 5 has a tennis ball and a handball.
- 5 has the handball and does a shooting feint.
- 6 sprints forward, initiates physical contact, and slightly pushes 5 back (E).
- 5 easily throws the tennis ball over 6 (F) as if he would play a banana pass.
- 6 turns around and tries to catch the tennis ball while it is in the air (G).

⚠ The players should react to the first sign immediately, start to sprint at once and start the action at top speed.

2. Stealing the ball 1-on-1

No. 7	Stealing the ball after observing the opponent	2	★
Equipment required:	4 cones and 1 handball per group of 2		

Course 1:

- The players make pairs.
- 1 dribbles a ball standing on the spot (A).
- 1 observes the dribbling and tries to steal the ball by doing a quick step forward with the right timing (B).
- 1 dribbles 1-2 meters (C), passes the ball back to 1, and starts the course over on the other side.
- The players switch tasks after 10 attempts.

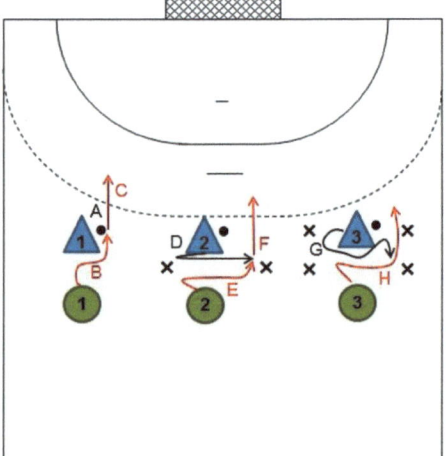

Course 2:
- The players make teams of 2 again; position two cones per team at a distance of 2-3 meters.
- 2 dribbles a ball while sidestepping from the left to the right cone and back (D).
- 2 observes the dribbling, moves along with 2, and then tries to steal the ball at the right time (E).
- 2 dribbles 1-2 meters (F), passes the ball back to 2, and starts the course over on the other side.
- The players switch tasks after 10 attempts.

Course 3:
- The players make teams of 2 again; define one narrow field per team with four cones.
- 3 dribbles a ball while moving freely within the field (G).
- 3 observes the dribbling, moves along with 3, and then tries to steal the ball at the right time (H).
- 3 dribbles 1-2 meters, passes the ball back to 3, and starts the course over on the other side.
- The players switch tasks after 10 attempts.

⚠ The ideal time for stealing the ball is when it bounces back up from the floor.

⚠ The defense player should steal the ball in such a way that he is able to control and dribble it.

Training of offensive defense systems in youth handball
1-on-1, small groups, man coverage, and offensive defense cooperation

No. 8	Ball stealing variants	2	★
Equipment required:	1 ball per group of 2		

Setting:
- The players form pairs, with each pair having one handball.

Course 1:

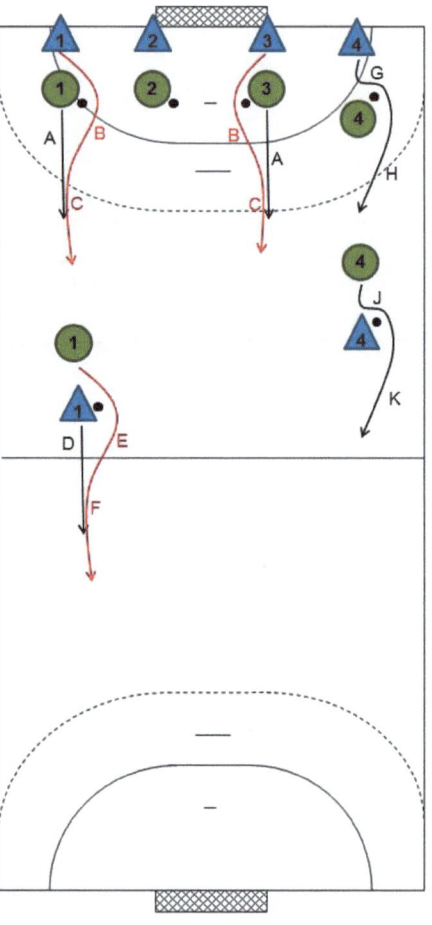

- The player in the front (1) starts to walk slowly and dribbles the ball with one hand in front of his body (A) (he must not change the dribbling hand).
- The player in the back (1) starts to jog slowly (A), overtakes on the side on which (1) dribbles the ball (B), and steals the ball while overtaking (C).

⚠ (1) should use the hand that is closer to (1) to steal the ball (i.e. he must not lean over to the other side!). If (1) overtakes (1) on the left side ((1) dribbles the ball with his left hand), (1) uses his right hand to steal the ball; if (1) overtakes (1) on the right side ((1) dribbles the ball with his right hand), (1) uses his left hand to steal the ball.

⚠ When (1) tries to steal the ball, he must adjust his timing, i.e. the ball must bounce back up from the floor as he tries to steal it.

- Once (1) has overtaken (1), he stops and starts to walk and dribble himself.
- The course starts over; this time, however, (1) tries to steal the ball (E and F).
- And so on.

Course 2:
- (1) now jogs slowly while he dribbles.

Course 3:
- Both players stand face-to-face.
- 4 dribbles the ball in front of his body while standing on the spot.
- 4 should wait for the right moment (when the ball bounces back up from the floor), then quickly make a step forward, and eventually steal the ball (G and H).
- 4 , who now has the ball, jogs a few meters and then turns around. The course starts over; this time, however, 4 tries to steal the ball from 4 (J and K).

No. 9	Stealing the ball in a predefined corridor	2	★
Equipment required:	4 cones and 1 handball per group of 2		

Setting:
- Make teams of 2 and define a playing field for each team with four cones.

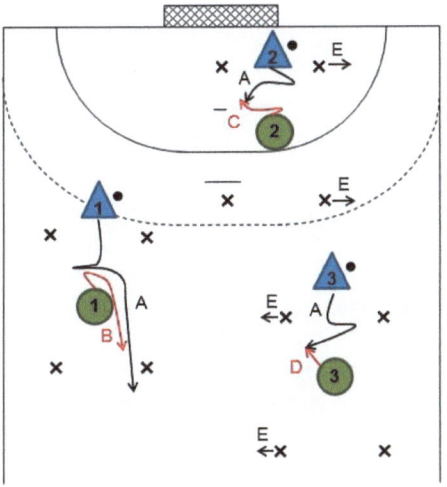

Course:
- The attacking players (1, 2, and 3 in the figure) dribble through the first two cones, then try to dribble through the field and leave it through the two backmost cones (A).
- The defense players (1, 2, and 3) try to stop the attacking players (B) and to steal the ball (C and D).
- Following the action, the attacking players move to the next defense player clockwise and start the course over.
- If a defense player has managed to steal the ball two times in a row, he may increase the size of his playing field (E).
- After two (three) full rounds (each attacking player has played two (three) attacks against each defense player), the players put the cones back to their initial positions and start the course over with new defense players.

⚠ The defense players should always focus on stealing the ball, but nevertheless obstruct the way to the cones in the back.

No. 10	Stealing the ball with varying attacking players	8	★
Equipment required:	2 ball boxes with sufficient number of handballs, 4 cones to define the playing field		

Setting:
- Define the defense zone with cones or existing lines; position a full ball box on the one side, and an empty ball box on the other side.

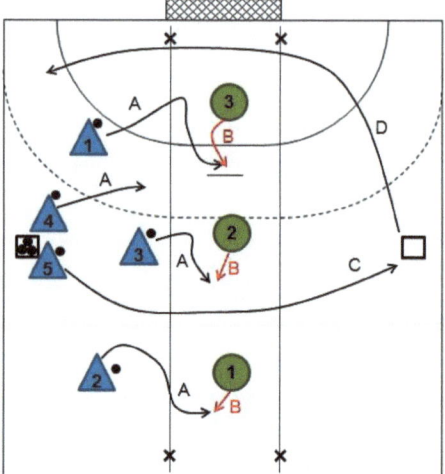

Course:
- Three players (1, 2, and 3 in the figure) start as defense players.
- The attacking players each pick up a ball and try to dribble through the defense zone (A) in order to put the ball in the empty box on the other side (C).
- Once they have put the ball in the box, the attacking players run back outside of the field (D) and pick up the next ball.
- The defense players try to interrupt the attacking players and to steal the ball (B) in order to roll it back behind the attacking players' starting line.
- How long does it take until the attacking players have put all their handballs in the empty box?
- Afterwards, the players start the next course with new defense players on the other side.

⚠ The defense players should always focus on stealing the ball, but nevertheless obstruct the way to the other half of the playing field.

No. 11	Stealing the ball and shooting at the goal	9	★

Equipment required: 4 cones, ball box with sufficient number of handballs

Setting:
- Define a playing field with cones (or existing lines) as shown in the figure and position a ball box on the side.

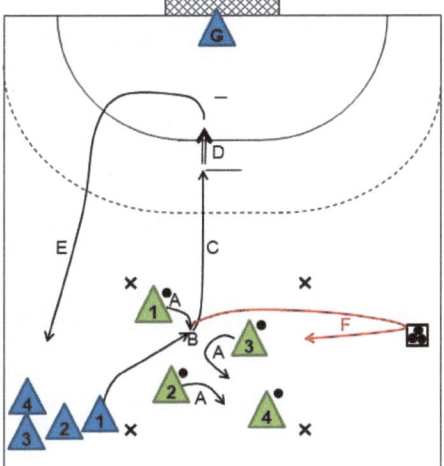

Course:
- Make two teams.
- One team starts in the field, with each player of this team having a ball.
- The other team stands outside of the field.
- On the coach's command, all the players in the field start to crisscross and to dribble their ball (A).
- ▲1 enters the field and tries to steal a ball (B).
- As soon as ▲1 has a ball, he approaches the goal (C) and shoots (D).
- If ▲1 scores a goal, his team gets a point.
- ▲1 lines up again (E).
- The player who lost his ball (▲1 in the figure), sidesteps back to the ball box immediately, picks up a new ball (F), and once more enters the field dribbling.
- As soon as ▲1 has left the field, ▲2 may enter the field and also try to steal a ball.
- The players switch tasks after five minutes (or five shots per player).
- Which team has shot the most goals?

⚠ The players in the field should try to keep their ball for as long as possible, without leaving the field.

⚠ Once a ball has been stolen, both players should start the subsequent action (shoot at the goal / pick up a new ball) immediately.

No. 12	Stealing the ball 1-on-1 on command	3	★★
Equipment required:	1 ball per group of 3		

Setting:
- ① stands in front of ▲1, at a distance of about 2-3 meters to ▲1.

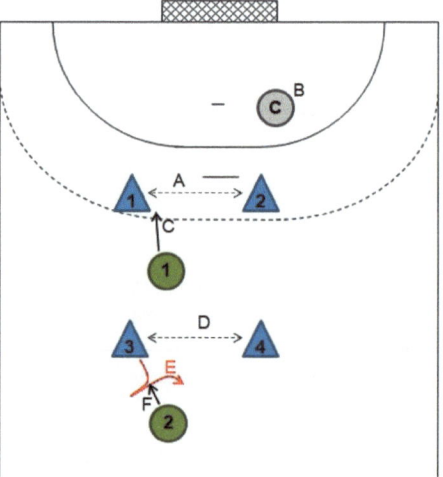

Course 1:
- ▲1 and ▲2 continuously pass a ball (A).
- As soon as the coach whistles (B), the ball should be passed to ▲1, and ▲1 starts to dribble the ball on the spot.
- ① makes 2-3 quick steps forward and steals the ball from ▲1 dribbling (C).
- Afterwards, ① moves to his initial position, in front of ▲2, and the players repeat the course. Change the players afterwards.

⚠ ① should allow the pass in any case and steal the ball only after ▲1 has started to dribble it.

⚠ The right time for the ball to be stolen is when it bounces back up from the floor.

Course 2:
- ▲3 and ▲4 continuously pass a ball (D).
- As soon as the coach whistles (B), the ball should be passed to ▲3.
- ▲3 immediately moves forward towards ②(E), without dribbling.
- ② makes a step forward towards ▲3 and tries to interrupt the attack at once (F).
- Afterwards, ② moves to his initial position, in front of ▲4, and the players repeat the course. Change the players afterwards.

Course 3:
- The players do the two previous exercises alternately.
- If ▲1 dribbles the ball, ① should try to steal it (C).
- If ▲1 does not dribble, ① should interrupt the attack (E and F).

3. Offensive 1-on-1 defense

No. 13	1-on-1 for three players	3	★
Equipment required:	3 cones per group of 3		

Setting:
- Position three cones per group of 3 as shown in the figure.

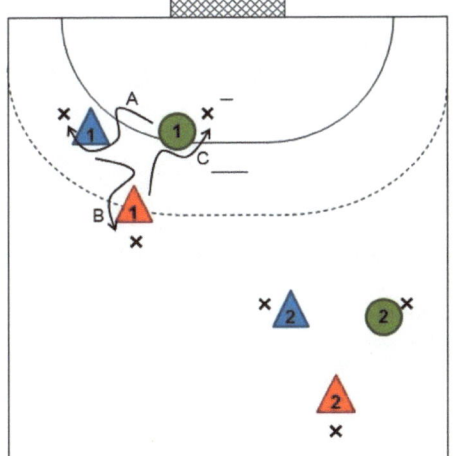

Course:
- 1 starts a 1-on-1 action against 1, without a ball, and tries to touch the cone with his foot/hand (A).
- 1 should sidestep quickly in order to obstruct the way to the cone and use his arms to hold 1 in front of him.
- As soon as 1 has touched the cone, cannot move any further / reach the cone, he steps back a bit, and 1 immediately starts his 1-on-1 action against 1 (B).
- As soon as 1 has touched the cone, cannot move any further / reach the cone, he steps back a bit, and 1 immediately starts his 1-on-1 action against 1 (C).
- The players keep going until each of them has performed 10 actions.

⚠ Immediately after their defense action, the defense players should adjust to the subsequent attack and start their 1-on-1 action.

⚠ The defense players should keep their arms slightly angled to hold the attacking players in front of their body.

⚠ If the attacking players do not succeed, the coach may initiate the change of tasks with a sign to make it a bit easier for them.

No. 14	Preventing passes	3	★
Equipment required:	4 cones and 1 handball per group of 3		

Setting:
- Divide the team into groups of 3. Each group of 3 has a ball (if the players cannot be divided into groups of 3, make groups of 4 with two attacking players taking turns).
- For each group, define a rectangle with four cones (see figure).

Course:
- ① starts in the rectangle as the defense player.
- ▲ enters the rectangle and tries to get in a good position to receive a pass from ▲ (A). The aim of ▲ is to receive the ball (E) and to leave the field crossing the backmost line of cones (D).
- ① offensively makes a step forward towards ▲ and moves along with ▲ in such a way that he cannot receive a pass from ▲ (B and C).
- While doing this, ① must make sure to always stand between ▲ and the finish line and to always quickly position himself in such a way that he obstructs the way to the finish line and, at the same time, prevents a pass to ▲ (C).
- If ▲ passes the ball nevertheless, ① tries to catch it.
- If ▲ has left the field with the ball or if ▲ has left the field without catching a pass, he turns around and starts the next action from the other side.
- The other teams of 3 do the drill in parallel in their respective rectangle field.
- After some time, the players of each group switch tasks.

⚠ The defense players should always position themselves between the attacking player and the finish line, but nevertheless observe the ball.

⚠ With quick sidesteps and backward steps, the defense players should try to keep up the distance to the attacking player while maintaining a proper defense posture.

Training of offensive defense systems in youth handball
1-on-1, small groups, man coverage, and offensive defense cooperation

⚠ The exercise may be adjusted to the players' level of performance by varying the field size.

⚠ The attacking players should try to break away in order to cross the line on the other side.

No. 15	Preventing a breakthrough with and without a ball	8	★
Equipment required:	12 cones, 2 vaulting boxes (upside down), ball box with sufficient number of handballs		

Setting:
- Define two corridors using cones and position two vaulting boxes upside down as goals.

Course:
- Make two teams, with one player per team playing defense against the respective other team.
- Assign a feeder/receiver to each team (3 and 4 in the figure).
- The first attacking players (1 and 2 in the figure) start by passing the ball to the feeder/receiver (A). Afterwards, they try to break away within the field (B), to receive the ball from the feeder/receiver (E) and to put it in the box (they may dribble, if necessary) (F). While doing this, the players may play several passes to the feeder/receiver.

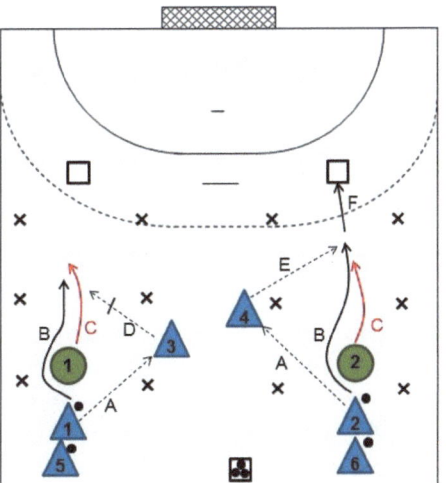

- 1 and 2 obstruct the way to the box (C) and try to prevent the passes (D) or to catch and steal the ball when the attacking player dribbles it.
- Once the ball is lost or has been put in the box, the next attacking player may start.
- Change the defense and offense players after a while.
- Which team has put the most balls in the box after a full course (i.e. each player playing defense once)?

⚠ The defense players should always position themselves between the attacking player and the finish line and try to observe the ball from this position.

⚠ The exercise may be adjusted to the players' level of performance by varying the field size.

No. 16	1-on-1 game on mats	8	★
Equipment required:	8 cones, 2 small gym mats, 2 ball boxes with sufficient number of handballs		

Setting:
- Position cones and small gym mats as shown in the figure.

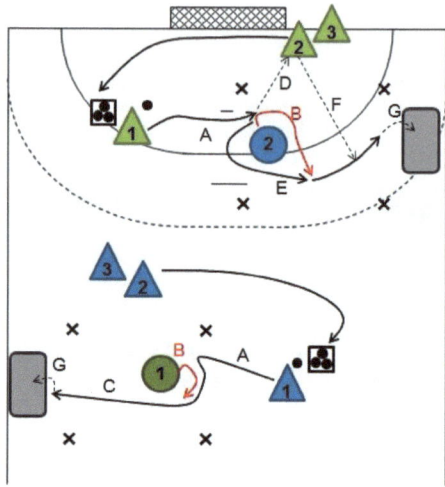

Course:
- Two teams (green and blue in the figure) play against each other.
- One player per team plays defense against the attacking players of the other team.
- On command, 🔺1 starts with a ball (A), tries to cross the field, and to put the ball on the small gym mat (G), 🔵1 defends against 🔺1 (B).
- At the same time, 🔺1 starts an attack against the defense player of the blue team.
- The attacking players may try to dribble past the defense player (C) or make use of a feeder/receiver (D, E, and F).
- The player who first put his ball on the mat gets a point for his team.
- On the next command, the former feeder/receiver starts the next action.
- Substitute the defense player after two rounds. Which team scores highest?

⚠ The defense players should always try to stand between the attacking player and the goal (small gym mat) and – depending on the situation – to steal the ball or prevent passes to the attacking player from this position.

Training of offensive defense systems in youth handball
1-on-1, small groups, man coverage, and offensive defense cooperation

No. 17	Three times 1-on-1 in a corridor	10	★
Equipment required:	8 cones, sufficient number of handballs		

Setting:
- Define three corridors with cones.

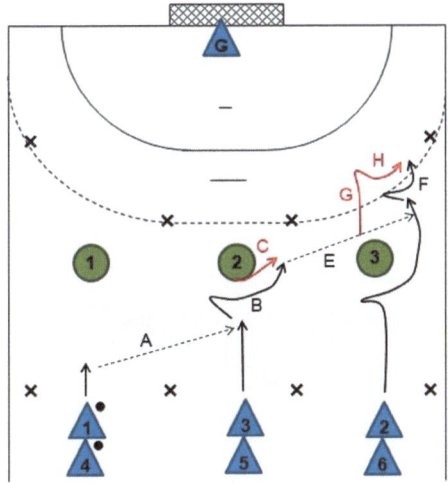

Course:
- 1, 2, and 3 play a free 3-on-3 game against 1, 2, and 3.
- While doing so, the attacking players are not allowed to leave their respective corridor.
- The attacking players try to score a goal by playing passes (A and E) and 1-on-1 attacks.
- The defense players initially move on a line and try to steal the ball as soon as one of the attacking players starts to dribble (C).
- If an attacking player moves without the ball, the respective defense player moves back (G), in order to be ready to defend and make a step forward as soon as the attacking player gets the ball and starts a 1-on-1 action (F and H).
- As soon as the attacking players have shot a goal or the defending players have successfully interrupted the attack, 4, 5, and 6 may start the next attack.
- Change the defense players after 10 attacks.

⚠ The defense players should focus on stealing the ball, but nevertheless obstruct the attacking players' way towards the goal.

Training of offensive defense systems in youth handball
1-on-1, small groups, man coverage, and offensive defense cooperation

No. 18	Two times 1-on-1 in a corridor	9	★
Equipment required:	6 cones, 2 ball boxes with sufficient number of handballs		

Setting:
- Use cones to define a corridor in the center of the field (see figure).

Course:
- 3 starts and dribbles through the first two cones (A).
- 1 and 2 try to get in a good position (B) for a pass from 3 (D).
- 1 and 2 defend against 1 and 2 in an offensive manner and try to prevent a pass (C).
- After receiving a pass, 1 and 2 keep playing until one of them has shot at the goal (E and F); 1 and 2 try to prevent a shot.
- If 3 cannot pass the ball before reaching the end of the corridor (G), 3 lines up again, and 1 and 2 start another attempt playing against 1 and 2, with 4 being the feeder. If a pass could be played, 3 switches tasks with the shooting player; the shooting player lines up next to the ball boxes again.

⚠ Switch the defense players at regular intervals.

⚠ The defense players should always position themselves between the attacking players and the goal and initially prevent a pass. If nevertheless a pass could be played to one of the attacking players, the defense players should prevent a shot at the goal and – if possible – steal the ball or force a bad pass.

No. 19a	1-on-1 with simultaneous observing of the player in ball possession	9	★★
Equipment required:	8 cones, sufficient number of handballs		

Setting:
- Define two corridors on the left and on the right side with cones (see figure).

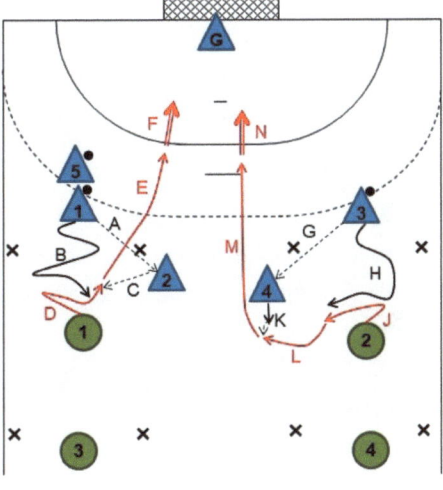

Course:
- ① plays the initial pass to ② (A) and then tries to get in a good position in the field (B) to receive a pass (C).
- ① tries to prevent the pass for as long as possible (D) and – ideally – to catch and steal the ball.
- If ① succeeds, he immediately approaches the goal (E) and shoots (F).
- Afterwards, the players do the same course on the right side (H and J).
- The feeder/receiver may also decide to put the ball on the floor (K) instead of passing it to the attacking player.
- This is the sign for the defense player to pick up the ball (L), approach the goal (M), and to shoot (N).
- After the shot, ① lines up behind ③ with a ball, ② lines up behind ⑤.
- ③ and ④ become the next defense players, ① and ③ line up for playing defense in the round after the next.
- Change the feeders/receivers after a while.

⚠ The defense players should defend against their direct opponent, but also observe the player in ball possession so that they can react immediately once the ball has been put on the floor. In order to do this, the defense players should move back to ball level at least.

No. 19b	**1-on-1 with simultaneous observing of the player in ball possession**	9	★★
Equipment required:	6 cones, sufficient number of handballs		

Setting:
- Divide the playing field in one center and two outer corridors (see figure).

Course:

- ③ and ④ are the feeders/receivers. They pass a ball in the center corridor (A and B).
- ① and ② play 1-on-1 (C) against ▲1 (E) and ▲2, without a ball, however. While doing this, the defense player should always try to position himself between his opponent and the goal, in order to prevent a pass (D).
- If nevertheless he received a pass, the attacking player approaches the goal and shoots (F).
- ① and ② move back in such a way that they can observe both their direct opponent and the ball (G).
- If ③ and ④ have played several passes but were unable to pass the ball to one of the attacking players, ③ or ④ drop the ball to the ground (H).
- This is the sign for the defense player, who is closer to the ball (② in the figure), to run towards the ball and pick it up (J).
- As soon as an attacking player has shot (F), a defense player has picked up the ball (J), or the ball got lost during the attack, the feeders/receivers start over with another ball and two new attacking players.
- Change the two defense players and the feeders/receivers after 10-15 defense actions.

⚠ The players should always position themselves between their direct opponent and the goal, but move back in such a way that they can also observe the ball.

⚠ The feeders/receivers in the center corridor should initially try to pass the ball to one of the attacking players before dropping it to the ground in the center corridor.

No. 20	1-on-1 with offensive defense lines – Moving back and attacking subsequently	7	★★★
Equipment required:	8 cones, ball box with sufficient number of handballs		

Setting:
- Define two playing corridors with four cones each.
- Provide a ball box with a sufficient number of handballs

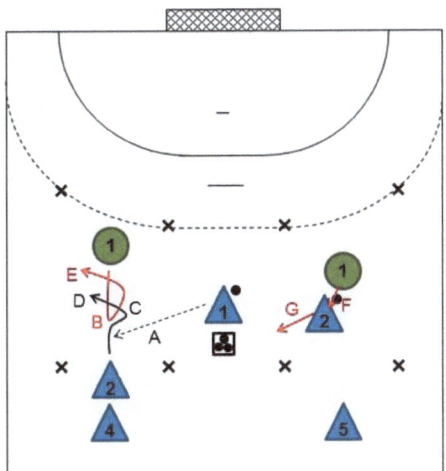

Course:
- ① starts each course standing near the 9-meter line.
- ① starts the course by passing the ball into the running path of ② (A).
- ① should clearly move towards the attacking player's movement (B).
- ② should now try to get past ① (either dribbling or within the 3-step rule) (C and D).
- ① moves backward immediately after the pass and moves along with ② (E).
    - If ① is able to directly defend against ② while moving backward, he should either tackle ② directly (F) or force ② to move out of the cone corridor (G).
- As soon as ② picks up the ball, ① has two options:
    - If ① stands close enough to ②, he should directly defend against ② (F) and try to force him out of the corridor (G) → This is the main objective.
    - If ① stands too far away from ②, he should keep up the distance and obstruct the way to prevent a shot.
- After the action, the second action starts on the right side.

⚠️ ① should try to slow down the running speed of ② and to directly defend against ② during the action. By moving back, the defending player should prevent a direct, full-speed 1-on-1 action of ②.

4. Catching and stealing the ball

No. 21	Series of shots with catching and stealing the ball	6	★
Equipment required:	2 cones, ball box with sufficient number of handballs		

Setting:
- Position two cones for the running path and a ball box as shown in the figure.

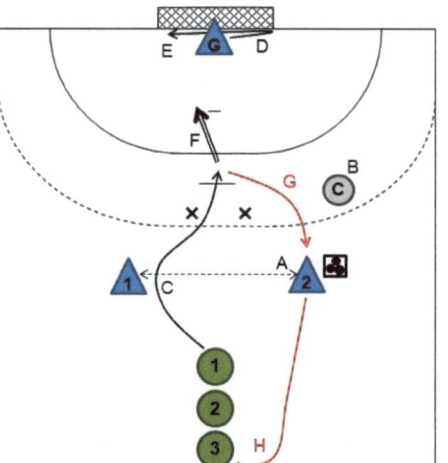

Course:
- 1 and 2 continuously pass a ball (A).
- As soon as the coach whistles (B), 1 starts and steals the ball passed by 1 and 2. 1 and 2 should allow the stealing!
- While 1 and 2 pass the ball, G does jumping jacks on the spot.
- As soon as 1 has caught the ball (C), G dynamically moves to the goalpost (D) and then moves to the right in order to save the ball (E) shot by 1 (F). 1 shoots freely at the right side of the goal.
- Afterwards, G moves back to the center of the goal and does jumping jacks again.
- Following the shot, the players repeat the course; once the ball has been stolen, 1 and 2 should pick up a new one and start over to pass.
- After the shot, 1 and 2 change positions (G), and 2 lines up again (H). The next player changes positions with 1; and so on.

⚠ The players should decide themselves on which side they steal the ball; they should try to steal it close to the player who is about to receive the pass, however (C).

⚠ The players should shoot at the right and left side of the goal alternately; the goalkeeper initially touches the respective goalpost on the opposite side.

Training of offensive defense systems in youth handball
1-on-1, small groups, man coverage, and offensive defense cooperation

No. 22	Series of shots with catching and stealing the ball 2	8	★
Equipment required:	4 cones, sufficient number of handballs		

Setting:
- Define the shooting positions on the right and left wing positions with cones; define the running paths near the center line with two cones as well.

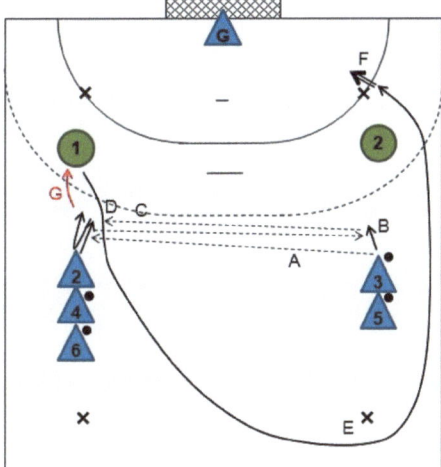

Course:
- 3 plays the initial pass to 2 (A); 2 does a slight piston movement, passes the ball back (B), and receives a return pass while doing another slight piston movement (C).
- 1 tries to catch and steal the second pass from 3 to 2 (D), runs around the right cone at the center line (E), approaches the goal, and finally shoots at the goal from the right wing position (F).
- In the meantime, 4 plays an initial pass to 3 in order to start the same course on the other side.
- 2 takes over the former position of 1 (G) for the next round on the left side, 1 lines up for the right back position.

No. 23a	Catching and stealing the ball from the defense position – Basic exercise	7	★
Equipment required:	6 cones, ball box with sufficient number of handballs		

Setting:
- Define a corridor in the center with cones as shown in the figure.

Course:
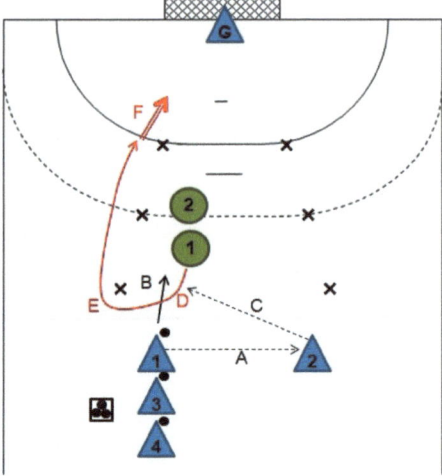
- 🔺1 plays the initial pass to 🔺2 (A), starts to run (B), and receives a return pass into his running path (C).
- 🟢1 defends offensively, in front of the 9-meter line, on the side of 🔺1.
- 🟢1 makes a step forward, catches and steals the ball (C) passed by 🔺2 (D), immediately runs around the line of cones on his side (E), dynamically approaches the goal, and eventually shoots (F).
- Afterwards, 🟢1 lines up for the defense again.
- 🔺2 moves forward a bit, and the players repeat the course with 🔺3 and 🔺2.
- And so on.

Variants:
- Change the defense side.

⚠ Change the players on the individual positions at regular intervals.

No. 23b	Catching and stealing the ball from the defense position – Advanced exercise	7	
Equipment required:	6 cones, ball box with sufficient number of handballs		

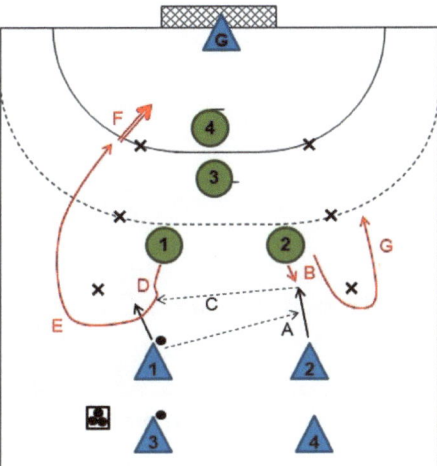

Setting:
- Define a corridor in the center with cones as shown in the figure.

Basic course:
- ① plays the initial pass into the running path of ② (A).
- ② dynamically steps forward towards ② and attacks him (B); ② should not be fouled, but be able to pass the ball to ①.
- ① should time his running movements in such a way that he always stands between ① and the goal, while keeping a distance of about 2-3 meters to ①.
- If ② passes the ball to ① (C), ① dynamically steps forward, catches and steals the ball (D), runs around the line of cones on his side (E), dynamically approaches the goal, and eventually shoots (F).

Extended course:
- ① and ② may play no more than four passes; after the fourth pass, one of the defense players must have caught and stolen the ball.
- If ② has caught and stolen the ball, he should run around the line of cones on his side and approach the goal dynamically (G).
- Following the individual actions, a new defense player (③) moves on to the unoccupied position.
- The players keep going. Change the defense and offense players after a while.

⚠ The defense players should do the running moves with quick steps and in a highly dynamic manner.

No. 24	Catching and stealing the ball following 1-on-1 actions	9	★★
Equipment required:	4 cones, sufficient number of handballs		

Setting:
- Position four cones as shown in the figure.

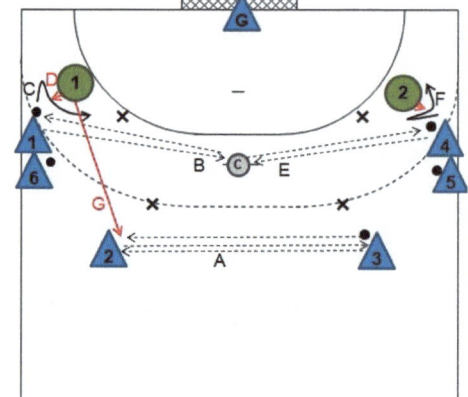

Course:

- 2 and 3 continuously pass a ball on the back positions (A).
- 1 passes the ball to the coach (B) and receives a return pass into his forward running path.
- 1 tries to get past 1 1-on-1 (C) and to shoot at the goal.
- 1 attacks 1 1-on-1 and tries to prevent the shot (D).
- Following the 1-on-1 action, 4 starts by playing the initial passes (E) and the 1-on-1 action against 2 (F).
- Immediately after his 1-on-1 action, 1 tries to catch and steal the ball that is passed by 2 and 3 (G).
- 1 may only try this during the ongoing 1-on-1 action of 4, since 6 will start his 1-on-1 action against him immediately afterwards.

⚠ The defense players should catch and steal the ball on the back position immediately after defending 1-on-1.

⚠ They should also make sure to catch the pass (A) close to the player who is about to receive it.

⚠ The players should switch positions at regular intervals.

| No. 25 | Catching and stealing the ball from the wing positions | 8 | ★★ |

Equipment required: 2 cones, sufficient number of handballs

Setting:
- Position two cones as shown in the figure.

Course:
- 2 passes the ball to 1, starts to run, and receives a return pass (A).
- Afterwards, 2 plays a long pass to 3 (B).
- 2 tries to get to the ball in time in order to catch and steal it (C).
- If 2 starts too early, 2 may also play a direct, long pass to 4 (D). 2 tries to catch (and steal) this ball, too.
- 1 and 2 switch positions (E) immediately after the long pass (B/D).
- The players do the course on the right and left side alternately so that the defense players have enough time to get back to their initial positions.

Variant:
- 2 crosses with 1, 1 then plays a long pass either to 3 or 4.

⚠ The defense players should find the right timing so that they are able to steal the ball without the attacking players recognizing their intention.

⚠ Change the defense players regularly.

⚠ The defense players should also make sure to catch the pass close to the player who is about to receive it.

5. Defense against the pivot in offensive defense systems

No. 26	Shielding off the pivot to prevent passes	7	★
Equipment required:	6 cones, 1 circle on the gym floor, and 1 handball		

Setting:
- Draw a circle on the court floor or use an already existing circle.
- Use tape to define a small circle or square in the center for the pivot's position.
- Define another circle outside (see figure).

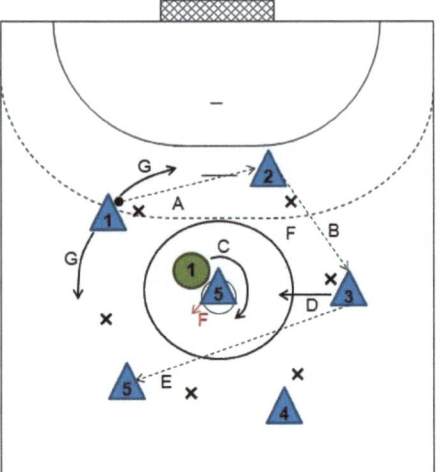

Course:
- One player starts as the pivot inside the circle, another player as the defense player. The other players stand around the outmost circle.
- The players outside of the circle pass a ball (A and B).
- ① tries to position himself in such a way between the pivot and the player in ball possession (C) that ⑤ cannot receive a pass (D).
- Change the defense players after several passing attempts; each player should have played defense at least once.
- Increase the difficulty level for the defense player gradually:
  - Initially, only passes from one position to the next (A and B) as well as return passes are allowed.
  - Then positions may be skipped (E). The defense player should react to these changes in speed.
  - The pivot initially stands inside the inner circle with both feet. Later on, the pivot is allowed to move more freely and to leave the inner circle with one foot (F). He should always keep one foot in the inner circle, however. With this variant, the defense player must move a lot more in order to shield off the pivot and to react to his movements.
  - During the last variant of the exercise, the attacking players may move along the outmost circle (G).

Training of offensive defense systems in youth handball
1-on-1, small groups, man coverage, and offensive defense cooperation

⚠️ If ① is unable to shield off ⑤ completely, he should at least try to catch the ball before ⑤.

⚠️ If there are too many players, the exercise may be done in two groups of four or five players standing around the outmost circle.

⚠️ ① should take quick steps, move in a highly dynamic manner, and always observe the player in ball possession.

No. 27	Shielding off the pivot to prevent passes 2	4	★
Equipment required:	2 cones and 1 handball per group of 4		

Setting:
- Make groups of four. Define a line with cones for each group.

Course:
- ② and ③ pass a ball (A).
- ① moves along the line (B) and tries to get in a good position for a pass.
- If ① is in a good position, ② or ③ pass the ball to ① (C).
- ① is the defense player, covering ①. If a pass is possible (C), ① should try to catch the ball before ① (D).
- The other teams of four do the drill in parallel (E).
- The players of each group should switch tasks after 2-3 minutes (approx. 10 actions).

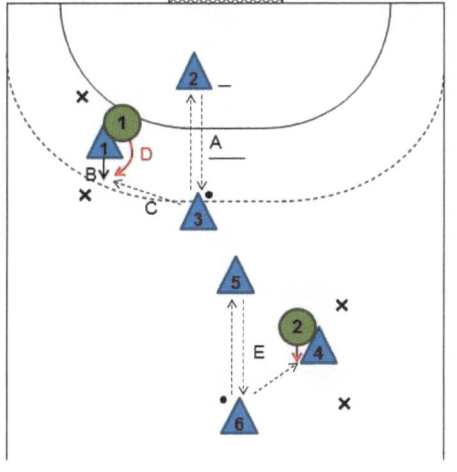

⚠️ The defense players should shield off the "pivots" and thus prevent a pass.

| No. 28 | Shielding off the pivot to prevent passes 3 | 7 | ★ |

Equipment required: 5 cones, ball box with sufficient number of handballs

Setting:
- Define the zone of the pivot with four cones.
- Position another cone in direction of the center line to define the running path for the second action.

Course:
- As soon as (c) whistles, 2 and 3 start to pass a ball (A).
- Both players should try to pass the ball to the pivot (1) (D).
- 1 may move freely within his zone and try to get in a good position for a pass (B). While doing so, he must not stay on the line, but is allowed to move within the field defined with cones.
- 1 should try to prevent a pass to 1 for as long as possible (C).
- If 1 nevertheless received a pass (D), 1 tries to turn around and shoot at the goal (E).
- As soon as 1 is about to shoot or (c) whistles one more time after some time has passed (10-20 seconds), 1 sprints around the cone in the back (F) and approaches the goal.
- 1 receives a second ball from (c) (G) and shoots at full speed (H).
- 1 becomes the new defense player, 2 becomes the new pivot, and 4 moves on to the next position (in the next round, 3 will become the new pivot and 5 will take over his position).

⚠ The objective of the defense player is to prevent a pass to the pivot until (c) whistles again.

⚠ The defense player should start the second action as soon as the pivot is about to shoot or (c) has whistled the second time.

6. Defense against the second pivot in offensive defense systems

No. 29	Moving along with the second pivot	7	★
Equipment required:	2 cones, ball box with sufficient number of handballs		

Setting:
- Use cones to define an existing line as finish line.

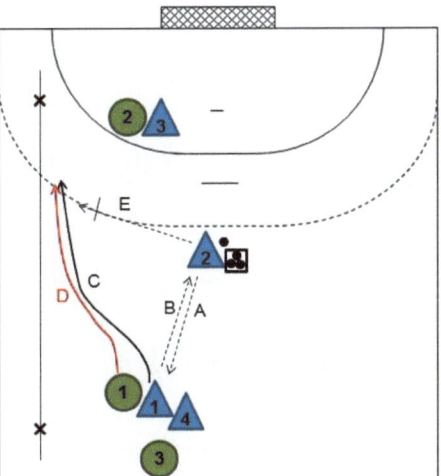

Course:
- 2 passes to 1 (A), and 1 passes back to 2 (B).
- After the second pass, 1 leaves his position (C) and tries to receive the ball at the finish line in order to put it on the floor behind the line.
- 1 moves along with 1 (D) and tries to prevent a pass from 2 to 1 (E).
- Following the action, 2 fetches a new ball from the ball box and the course starts over on the other side, with 2 defending against 3 who will leave his position.
- 1 lines up for the former position of 3, 1 waits outside of the field in order to substitute 2 after his defense action.
- 3 takes over the position of 1 and starts the next defense action against 4 on the left side.
- If there are many players, make several groups and define further lines so that the groups can do the course in parallel.

⚠ The defense player should move along with the running player in such a way that he always stands between the finish line and the attacking player. While doing so, he should initiate physical contact in order to force his opponent away and to be able to catch and steal the ball (E).

⚠ Change the feeder/receiver (2) at regular intervals.

No. 30	**Moving along with the second pivot and playing 2-on-2**	9	★
Equipment required:	4 cones, 2 ball boxes with sufficient number of handballs		

Setting:
- Use cones to define a corridor in the center of the field (see figure).

Course:

- 3 starts and dribbles through the first two cones (A).
- 1 and 2 try to get in a good position (B) for a pass from 3 (D).
- 1 and 2 defend against 1 and 2 in an offensive manner and try to prevent a pass.
- 1 and 2 may use the entire half of the playing field; if a player runs to the other side, the defense player should move along with him (C).
- After the pass (D), 1 and 2 may keep playing freely until one of them has shot at the goal (E); 1 and 2 try to prevent the shot.
- If 3 has arrived at the two foremost cones (F), he should pick up the ball and pass it to 1 or 2 within three seconds.
- If the attacking players do not succeed, 1 and 2 play another attack with 4 being the feeder; 3 lines up again.
- If 3 was able to pass the ball, he switches tasks with the shooting player; the shooting player lines up again.

⚠ Switch the defense players at regular intervals.

⚠ The defense players should always position themselves between the attacking players and the goal and initially prevent a pass. If nevertheless a pass could be played to one of the attacking players, the defense players should prevent a shot at the goal and – if possible – steal the ball or force a bad pass.

⚠ Confine the playing field depending on the players' level of performance.

| No. 31a | Moving along with the second pivot from the wing position | 7 | ★ |

Equipment required: 4 cones, ball box with sufficient number of handballs

Setting:
- Position cone goals as shown in the figure.

Course:
- 3 and 4 continuously pass a ball (A and B).
- Anytime while 3 and 4 pass the ball, one of the wing players (2 in the figure), tries to become the second pivot (C).
- The defending wing player (2) should obstruct the way and move along with 2 (D) so that he cannot receive a pass from 4 or 3 (E).
- If nevertheless the running player receives a pass (E), 2 should try to prevent him from turning around and shooting (F).
- Following the action, 3 and 4 start over passing a ball. 2 and 2 move back to their initial positions, and the course starts over.

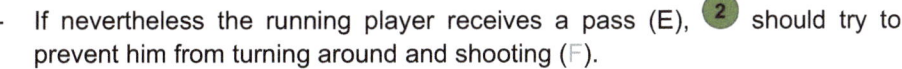

⚠ The defense players should position themselves in such a way that they obstruct the wing player's way and then move along with him to prevent a pass, if possible.

⚠ The defense players should vary their initial positions (at the 6-meter line, in the center of the cone goal, near the cone in the front).

⚠ The players should switch positions at regular intervals.

| No. 31b | Moving along with the second pivot from the wing position and preventing a breakthrough | 7 | ★★ |

Equipment required: 2 cones, 2 ball boxes with sufficient number of handballs

Setting:
- Use two cones to divide the playing field in two halves.

Course:

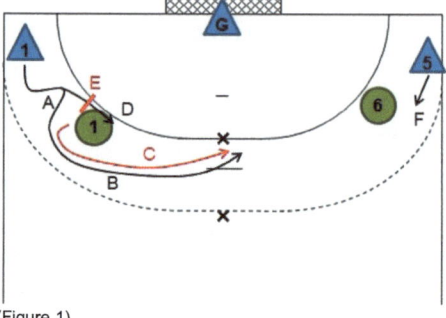

- 1 starts from the wing position (A) and tries to get to the 6-meter line, behind 1 (B).
- 1 moves along with 1 and tries to prevent the wing player from getting to the 6-meter line by pushing 1 towards the cones (C).

(Figure 1)

⚠ 1 should prevent 1 from getting to the 6-meter line in any case (D) by obstructing the way between himself and the 6-meter line (E).

- Repeat the course on the other side (F); and so on.
- Change the defense players after several rounds.

⚠ 1 must not tackle 1, but push him in front of his body and use his arms to prevent him from getting through.

Extension:

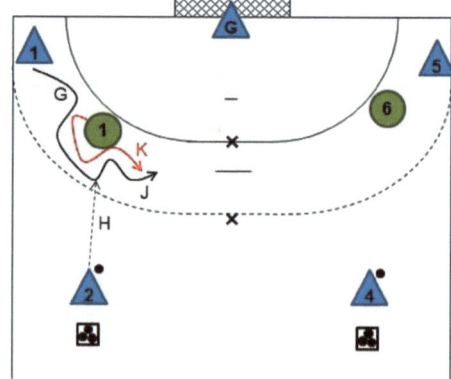

- 1 starts from the wing position (G) and receives a pass from 2 into his running path (H).
- 1 may now try to break through and to shoot at the goal (J).
- 1 should defend in the back and may also try to catch and steal the ball.
- If he cannot steal the ball, he should try to prevent a breakthrough.

(Figure 2)

⚠ 1 should vigorously force 1 to move towards the 9-meter line. If 1 has been forced to move out of the 9-meter zone, the action is over.

Training of offensive defense systems in youth handball
1-on-1, small groups, man coverage, and offensive defense cooperation

No. 32	Moving along with the second pivot from the back positions and defending against two pivots	9	★★

Equipment required: 2 cones, 2 ball boxes with sufficient number of handballs

Setting:
- Define the playing field with two cones.

Course:
- ① passes to ② (A).
- After the pass, ① runs towards the 6-meter line (B).
- ② moves along with ① and tries to prevent a pass (C).
- As soon as ① is on his way, ② and ③ pass the ball on the back positions (D) and try to play a pass to one of the pivots, i.e. ① or ⑥ (E).
- ① and ② try to prevent a pass to one of the pivots as long as they can by communicating properly in case of positional changes of the two pivots (F), and taking/handing over (G) as necessary.
- As soon as one of the pivots has shot at the goal or the defense players have won the ball, ② and ③ start the course over, with ② running towards the 6-meter line.
- ③ becomes a defense player against ②, ② keeps defending against the first pivot, ① positions himself on the left side and becomes a defense player in the third round.

(Figure 1)

(Figure 2)

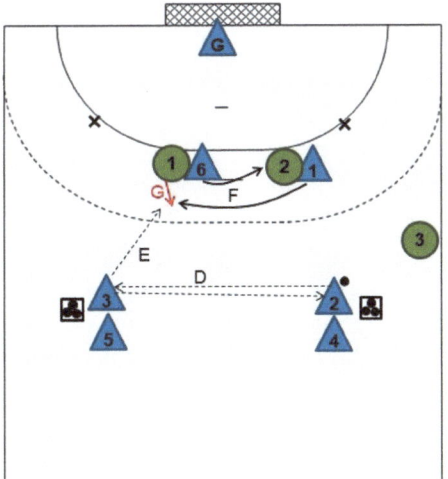

⚠ Switch the defense players after several actions.

Category: Small group defense

1. Cooperation across the width of the defense zone

No. 33	2-on-2 competition	8	★
Equipment required:	12 cones, 4 vaulting boxes (upside down), 2 ball boxes with sufficient number of handballs		

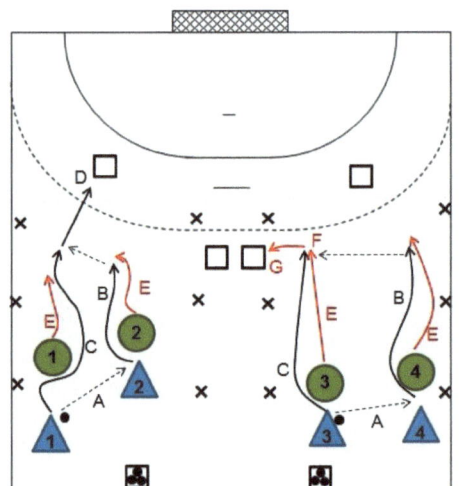

Setting:
- Define two corridors with cones.
- Position goal boxes and ball boxes, each of the latter with the same number of handballs for both teams (see figure).

Course:
- Make two teams; the attacking players in the first corridor make a team with the defending players in the second corridor.
- In both corridors, the players play 2-on-2 in parallel (A, B, C, and E). The attacking players should try to put the ball in the box on the other side (D).
- If the defense players catch and steal a ball (F) or if the attacking players make a technical mistake, the players of the defending team may put the ball in their own box (G).
- As soon as the first ball box is empty, count the points of defense and offense. The players switch tasks afterwards and start the course over.
- Which team gets the most points in two rounds?

⚠ Adjust the corridor width to the players' level of performance.

| No. 34 | 2-on-2 defense in a corridor and supporting each other in case of a breakthrough | 9 | ★ |

Equipment required: 8 cones, sufficient number of handballs

Setting:
- Define a corridor with cones.

Course:
- 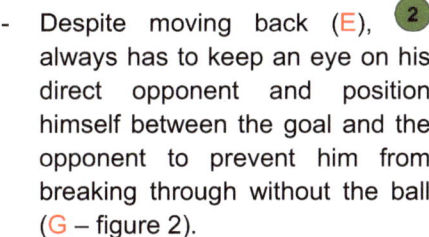 and 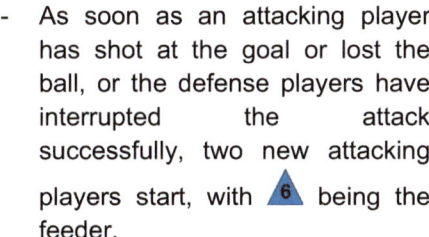 play 2-on-2 against ▲1 and ▲2, initially without a ball.
- The feeder standing outside the corridor (▲3) has a ball and starts dribbling (A).
  If he is able to pass the ball into the corridor (B), the direct defense player (▲1) should try to prevent a breakthrough (C and D).
- The second defense player (▲2) moves back to ball level (E) in order to support his teammate in case of a breakthrough (F).
- Despite moving back (E), ▲2 always has to keep an eye on his direct opponent and position himself between the goal and the opponent to prevent him from breaking through without the ball (G – figure 2).
- As soon as an attacking player has shot at the goal or lost the ball, or the defense players have interrupted the attack successfully, two new attacking players start, with ▲6 being the feeder.
- Change the feeders and the defense players after 10-15 defense actions.

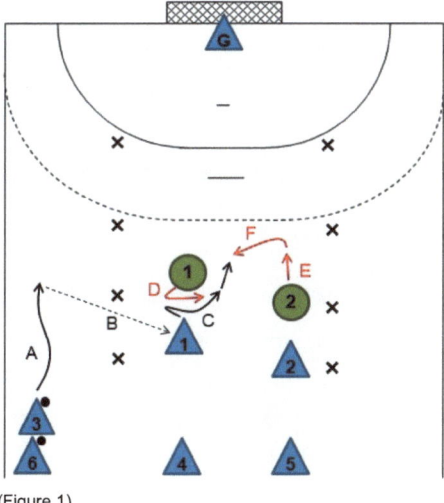

(Figure 1)

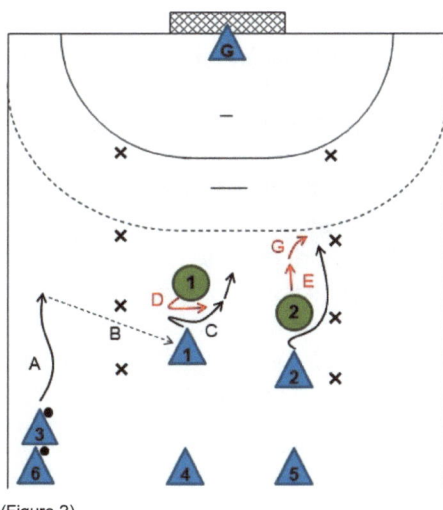

(Figure 2)

⚠ The players should always position themselves between their direct opponent and the goal, but move back so far that they can also observe the ball and support their teammate in case of a breakthrough.

No. 35	2-on-2 defense in a corridor with handing/taking over in case of crossing movements	10	★★

Equipment required:	8 cones, sufficient number of handballs

Setting:
- The players make groups of 5 (further players will be added to the offense).
- Define a field for each group with four cones (see figure).

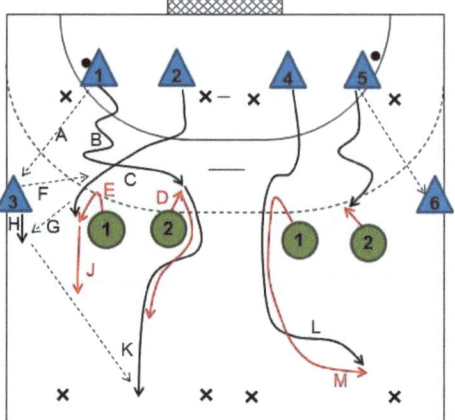

Course:
- ▲1 starts and passes the ball to ▲3 (A). Following this, ▲1 and ▲2 try to break away within the field and to get in a good position for a pass (B).
- ●1 and ●2 try to prevent a pass.
- If the attacking players cross (C), the defense players should communicate with each other, ●2 takes over ▲1 (D), and ●1 moves towards ▲2 (E).
- If a pass is possible (F), the defense players try to prevent a breakthrough, and the ball should be passed back to ▲3 (G). ▲3 may move along at the side of the field (H).
- The defense players should keep moving along with the attacking players (J).
- If the attacking team gets the ball and crosses the backmost line (K), they get a point. The course starts over with the next attacking team.
- The other groups do the course in parallel.
- If an attacking player overlaps a defense player (L), the respective defense player should move along with him (M).
- Change the tasks within the individual groups after 10 defense actions (new feeder/receiver, new defense players).

⚠ The defense players should communicate and coordinate the handing/taking over and quickly move to the respective attacking player.

⚠ In order to do the handing/taking over properly, the defense players must move back to ball level already when covering their respective opponent.

Extension:
- The attacking players may dribble and change positions (crossing with the ball). In this case, the defense players should also communicate with each other and coordinate the handing/taking over, if necessary.

| No. 36 | 2-on-2 defense in a corridor with and without a ball against crossing moves and overlapping | 10 | ★★ |

Equipment required: 6 cones, ball box with sufficient number of handballs

Setting:
- Position six cones for a corridor as shown in the figure.
- Provide a ball box for playing passes.

Basic course:
- 1 and 2 start the course by doing running feints (A and B). They should try to get past 1 and 2 in such a way that they get in a good position for a pass (C) and subsequently can shoot at the goal.

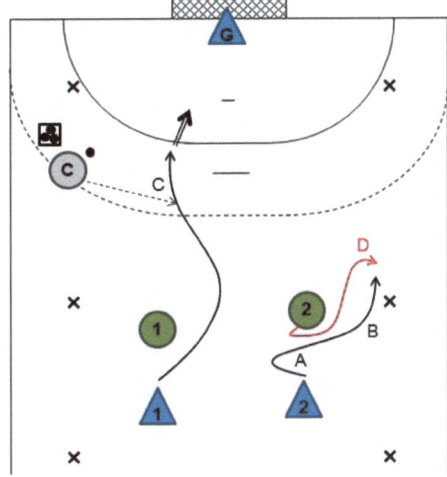

(Figure 1)

- 1 and 2 try to prevent the attacking players from breaking away through quick steps and by using their arms ("shock absorbers" (see below)) (D) and to interrupt the attack and/or delay the shot for as long as possible.
- If C passes the ball, but a direct shot is not possible, 1 and 2 should play 2-on-2 until one of them is in a good position for a shot.
- Afterwards, the former attacking players become the defense players and the next two attacking players start the course over.

(Basic) Rule no. 1:
- Each defense player must stick with his attacking player and cover him consistently in order to prevent a pass.

Shock absorbers:
- The defense player should hold the respective attacking player in front of his body, but without tackling him. Through little pushes, he should force him to move away in order to keep up a certain distance and to be able to reposition himself over and over.
- The attacking player must not be pushed hardly.

Rule no. 2 (G) (for crossings):
- In the beginning, the attacking players should be followed (E and F). As soon as the attacking players start a crossing, ① and ② should communicate loudly and take over the respective attacking player (H and J).

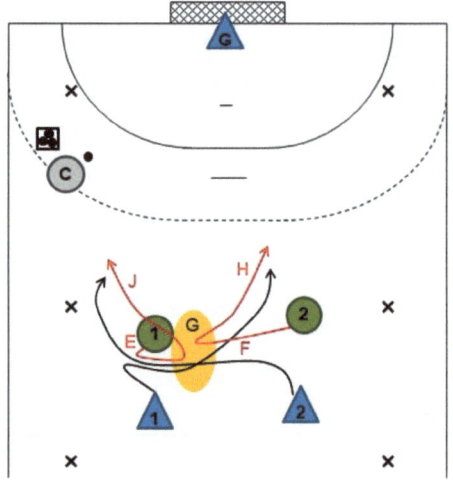

(Figure 2)

Rule no. 3 (N) (an attacking player leaves his position and runs behind the defense line):
- In the example, ▲1 leaves his position and runs towards the gap between ① and ② (K).
- ② does not join the crossing but keeps his position or move along on a parallel path (L).
- In this case, ① stays with ▲1 and covers the zone in the back, towards the goal (M).
- ① and ② should nevertheless keep communicating with each other in order to cover the zone between them (N).

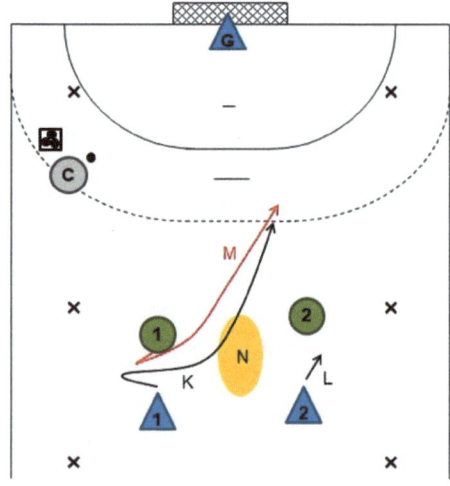

(Figure 3)

⚠ You may adjust the size of the corridor to the attacking and defending players' level of performance.

No. 37	2-on-2 switch game	12 (14)	★★
Equipment required:	4 small gym mats, 1 handball		

Setting:
- Put small gym mats on the floor as targets (see figure).

Course 1:
- 🔺1 and 🔺2 play 2-on-2 against 🔵1 and 🔵2. They should try to put the ball on the mat behind 🔵1 and 🔵2.
- While doing this, the attacking players should try to outnumber the defense players through crossings (A to C).
- The defense players should communicate and coordinate the taking/handing over and thus try to prevent a breakthrough (D).
- As soon as the attacking team has put the ball on the mat or the defending team has won the ball, 🔵1 and 🔵2 become the new attacking team and start an attack against 🔵3 and 🔵4. 🔺1 and 🔺2 become defense players.

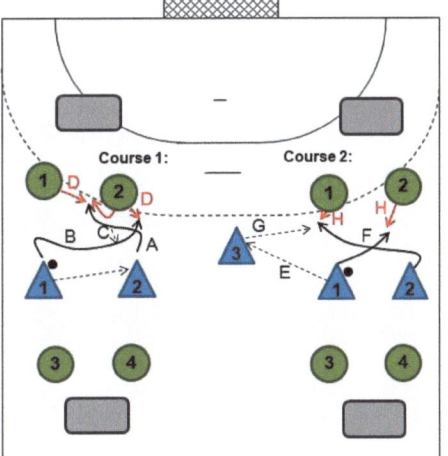

Course 2:
- The basic course remains the same as course 1.
- In addition, 🔺3 serves as feeder/receiver for the respective attacking team (E and G); i.e. the attacking players may also pass the ball to 🔺3 (E), cross without the ball (F), and then receive a pass from 🔺3 (G).
- The defense players should also communicate and coordinate the taking/handing over of the attacking players in case there is a crossing without the ball.
- Change 🔺3 after several passes.

⚠️ If the attacking team plays a crossing, the defense players should communicate permanently and coordinate the taking over.

⚠️ Following the defense action, the defense players should adjust to the new situation immediately, become the attacking players, and start their attack towards the other side.

| No. 38 | 3-on-3 defense | 6 | ★★ |

Equipment required: 2 small gym mats, 2 cones, item to divide the playing field in two halves

Setting:
- Divide the court in two halves.
- Position a small gym mat in the goal zone of each half (at a certain distance to the 6-meter line, as shown in the figure).

Course:
- The players play 3-on-3 on each half of the playing field. Following the initial passes (A and B), the attacking team (1, 2, and 3) should try to approach the mat 1-on-1 (C) or try to break through directly or through a parallel piston movement (D and E) in order to put the ball on the mat.

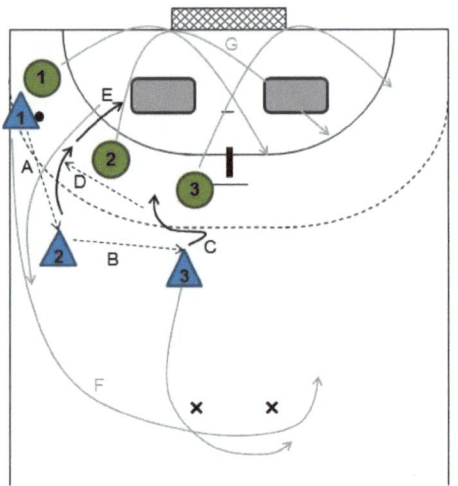

- The defense players 1, 2, and 3 should stand between the goal and their opponents, defend 1-on-1, and support each other in case of a breakthrough.
- If the attack was successful and the ball is on the mat, the attacking players run around the cones (F) and may start another attack on the other half of the field.
- The defense players should touch the respective goalpost (G) and position themselves on the other side.
- If 1, 2 and 3 could prevent the attacking players from putting the ball on the mat, the teams switch tasks. The defense players run around the cones (F) and may start the next attack; the former attacking players touch the respective goalpost and then become the defending team on the other half of the field.
- Which team gets the most points (ball on the mat)?
- Allow crossings in the second round – the defense players should communicate with each other accordingly.

⚠️ After getting a point or winning the ball, the players should adjust to the new situation and start the subsequent action at once.

Variant:
- Limit the time for each attack (20 seconds after the ball has been put on the mat); if the time is over, the defending team gets a point.

Training of offensive defense systems in youth handball
1-on-1, small groups, man coverage, and offensive defense cooperation

2. Cooperation throughout the depth of the defense zone

No. 39	Shielding off two pivots to prevent passes from the back positions	10	★
Equipment required:	4 foam beams, 1 ball box with sufficient number of handballs		

Setting:
- Define two corridors using foam beams (see figure).

Course:
- 3 starts and passes a ball to 2 (A).
- 1 tries to get in a good position for a pass (B).
- 1 tries to prevent a pass to 1 by moving along with 1 and shielding him off against passes (C and D).
- 3 should prevent diagonal passes to 5 on the other side (E and F).
- If 2 cannot play a pass, he passes the ball back to 3 (G), and 3 passes to 4 (H).
- Repeat the course on the other side.
- 1 positions himself between the player in ball possession and 1 (K), particularly to prevent 1 (J) from overlapping (J).
- If the pivot makes a step forward (N), he should be followed as well (M).
- The defense players should always try to prevent a pass to the pivots (O and P), so that 4 is forced to pass the ball back to 3.
- If one of the pivots nevertheless received a pass (not shown in the figure), he should try to shoot at the goal. Provide a new ball in this case.

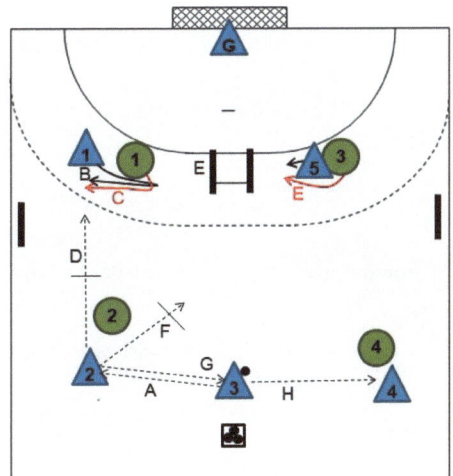

(Figure 1)

(Figure 2)

- Substitute the defense players and the pivots after 10 passes from ③ to ② or ④.

Extension:
- Allow return passes and direct passes on the back positions, from ② to ④ and vice versa; ③ may also pass the ball to one of the pivots.

⚠ ② and ④ should support their teammates by trying to block passes to the pivots.

No. 40	2-on-2 against a back position player and a pivot	7	★
Equipment required:	4 cones, ball box with sufficient number of handballs		

Setting:
- Define the playing field with four cones (see figure).

Course:
- ② and ① (pivot) play 2-on-2 against ① and ②. ③ and ④ serve as feeders/receivers for ②.

(Figure 1)

- ② may pass the ball to the feeders/receivers any number of times (A). The feeders/receivers may only pass the ball back to ②, but not to the pivot (①).
- If ② receives the ball, ② should offensively step forward towards him, defend any breakthrough attempts (B) 1-on1 (C) and also try to prevent or block a pass to the pivot.
- Initially, ① covers the pivot, moves along with him, and shields him off against passes.
- During the game, two difficult situations may arise for the defense players:
  o ② manages to break through 1-on-1 against ② (D). In this case, ① must quickly decide to support his teammate (E) and to leave his position next to the pivot. As a result, ② must move back to the pivot immediately (F) to prevent a pass (G) (see figure 1). If the attacking players change positions, ① and ② should communicate with each other accordingly.

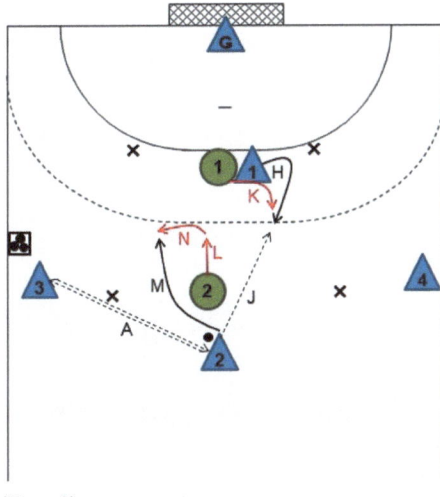
(Figure 2)

- ○ 1 may break away at the 6-meter line (H) and receive a pass from 2 (J). 1 should now try to prevent 1 from breaking through towards the goal (K). 2 moves back a bit (L) to further observe the ball and his opponent. If 2 now tries to get in a good position for playing a double pass and approaching the goal (M), 2 should always try to position himself between 2 and the goal (N) (figure 2). The defense players ideally force the pivot to pass the ball back to 2 or one of the feeders/receivers.
- As soon as the attack is over, 3 and 4 become the next attacking players, and two new feeders/receivers enter the field.

No. 41	3-on-3 against two back position players and the pivot	9	★
Equipment required:	2 cones, sufficient number of handballs		

Setting:
- Define the playing field with two cones.

Course:
- Make teams of 3 (if there are players left, one player may play defense two times in a row).
- The first team of 3 (①, ②, and ③) initially defends 10 attacks, whereas the other players take turns for the attacks.
- The teams play 3-on-3 with feeders/receivers on both sides. One player is the pivot.

(Figure 1)

- ①, ②, and ③ initially play defense with a clear, fixed coverage of their respective opponent.
- ② and ③ make a step forward as soon as the respective back player receives the ball, defend 1-on-1, and try to prevent or block passes to the pivot (A).
- If a back player manages to break through (③ in the figure), ① should decide to support his teammate (B).
- The respective defending player (③) must move back immediately (C) and try to prevent a pass to the pivot.
- ② should also observe the ball and his opponent and may support his teammates to defend against the pivot, if necessary (not in the figure).

- If the pivot nevertheless receives a pass (D), the defense players should try to prevent him from breaking through (E).
- The foremost defense line moves back a bit (F) in order to further observe the ball and the opponents and to support their teammates defending against the pivot, if necessary.
- At the same time, the defense players must prevent the back players from breaking through without the ball. In order to do this, the respective defense players, ② and ③, should always maintain their positions between the goal and their respective opponent (G).

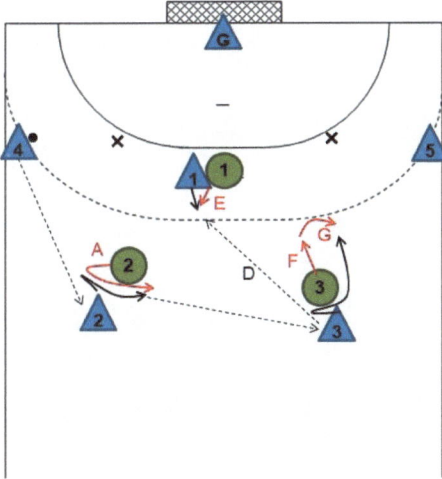

(Figure 2)

- The defense players ideally force the pivot to pass the ball back to one of the back position players.
- After 10 attacks, a new team of 3 becomes the defending team. Which team prevents the most goals?

⚠ The defense players should communicate with each other and coordinate the taking/handing over in case of positional changes.

| No. 42 | Defending against the back position players and the pivot 4-on-4 | 9 | ★ |

Equipment required: 2 foam beams, 1 handball

Setting:
- Define the playing corridor with the foam beams (see figure).

Course:
- The players play 4-on-4.
- The defense players play with a clear, fixed coverage of their respective opponent.
- 2, 3, and 4 make a step forward as soon as the respective back player receives the ball, defend 1-on-1 (A), and try to prevent or block passes to the pivot.

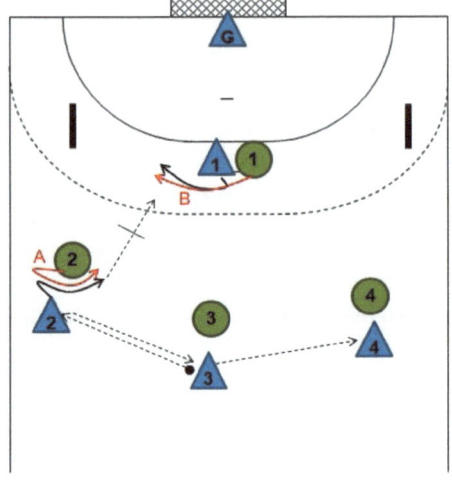

(Figure 1)

- 1 moves along with the pivot (B) and shields him off against passes from the back players.
- If a back player (4 in the figure) manages to break through (C), 1 should decide to support his teammate (D).
- The respective defending player (4) must move back (E) and try to prevent a pass to the pivot.
- If the pivot nevertheless receives a pass (not shown in the figure), 1 tries to prevent him from breaking through. The other defense players try to prevent the back players from breaking away without the ball. The defense players ideally force the pivot to pass the ball back to the players in front of the foremost defense line.
- Change the defense players after 10 attacks. Which defense team prevents the most goals?

(Figure 2)

Training of offensive defense systems in youth handball
1-on-1, small groups, man coverage, and offensive defense cooperation

No. 43a	Shielding off and communicating: Pivot standing at the 6-meter line	7	
Equipment required:	2 cones, 1 handball		

Setting:
- Define the playing field with two cones as shown in the figure.

⚠ The two defense players should keep communicating loudly during the defense task.

Course:

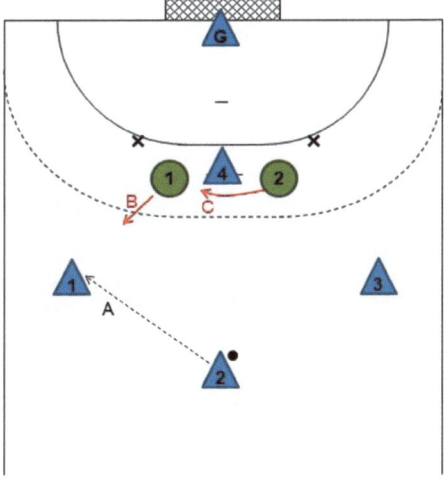

- 1, 2, and 3 pass a ball. While doing so, they should also do slight piston movements. 2 is the feeder/receiver and must not pass the ball to the pivot (4).
- During the course, 4 stands in the center, next to the 7-meter line.

(Figure 1)

- 2 starts the course and passes the ball to 1 (A).
- 1 makes a step forward towards 1 (B), 2 moves next to 4 (C) in order to shield him off against a pass from 1 by putting his arm around 4 (see figure 3).
- 1 passes the ball back to 2 (D).
- As soon as the pass has been played, 1 immediately moves back towards 4 (E), and 2 moves to the right side a bit (F).
- 2 passes the ball to 3 (G). As soon as the pass has been played:
  - 1 moves to 4 so that he cannot receive a pass from 3 (H);
  - 2 steps forward towards the movement path of 3 (J).

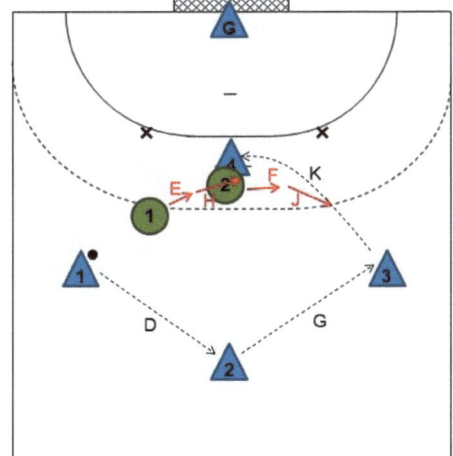

(Figure 2)

- If 🔺1 or 🔺3 nevertheless pass the ball to 🔺4 (K), they may try to play a pass to 🔺4, and 🔺4 may try to shoot at the goal.

⚠️ In the beginning, the attacking players should only pass the ball from one position to the next. In the further course, 🔺2 may also choose to play a return pass.

- Change the defense players after several rounds. Which team of two prevents the most passes to the pivot?

The shield-off posture (see figure 3):
- The players should stand next to the pivot and use their arm to shield him off against a pass.

(Figure 3)

No. 43b	Shielding off and communicating: Pivot standing offensively between the 7- and 9-meter lines	7	
Equipment required:	2 cones, 1 handball		

Setting:
- Define the playing field with two cones as shown in the figure.

Course:
- ① makes a step forward towards the player in ball possession.
- ② tries to force ④ to move out of the 9-meter zone as far as he can (L).

⚠ ② must not push ④ away vigorously.

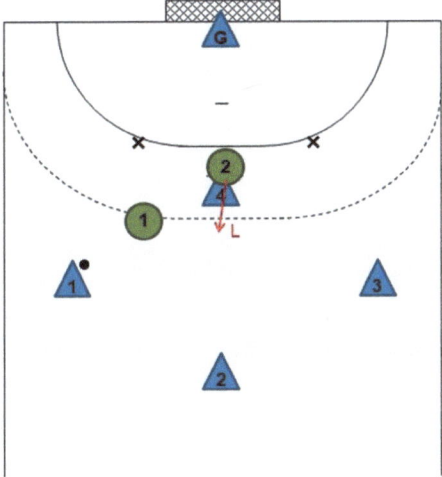

(Figure 1)

- As soon as ② passes the ball to ③ (D und G):
  - ① immediately moves back, behind ④ (M);
  - ② steps forward towards the movement path of ③ (N).
- ① actively works against ④, so that ④ is being pushed as far away from the 6-meter line as possible (L), and ① stands between ④ and the 6-meter line.

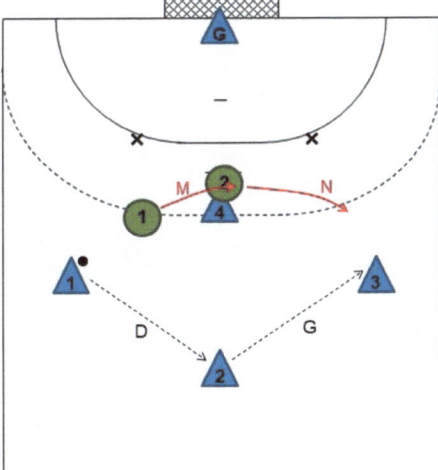

(Figure 2)

| Nr.43c | **Shielding off and communicating: Pivot standing on the ball side** | 7 | ★★ |

Equipment required: 2 cones, 1 handball

Setting:
- Define the playing field with two cones as shown in the figure.

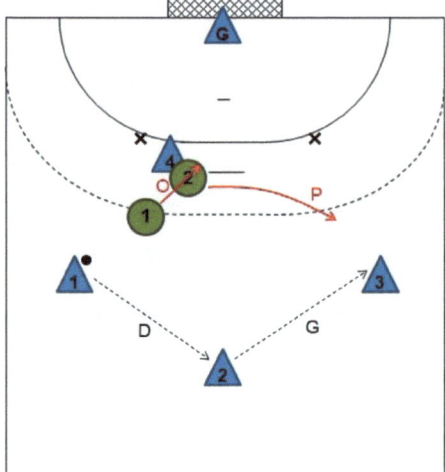

Course:
- ① makes a step forward towards the player in ball possession.
- ② shields off the zone next to ④, to prevent a pass (see figure 3 in exercise 43a).
- As soon as ② passes the ball to ③ (D und G):
  - ① moves backward immediately until he stands right in front of ④ (O);
  - ② actively steps forward towards the movement path of ③ (P).

No. 43d	**Shielding off and communicating: Pivot standing on the non-ball side**	7	★★
Equipment required:	2 cones, 1 handball		

Setting:
- Define the playing field with two cones as shown in the figure.

Course:
- ① makes a step forward towards the player in ball possession.
- ② stands next to ④ (between ① and ④), so that a direct pass is not possible.

⚠ ② should always touch ④ with his hand so that he notices immediately when ④ is about to move away.

- As soon as ② passes the ball to ③ (D und G):
  - ① immediately moves back and next to ④ (Q), and shields him off to prevent a pass from ③;
  - ② steps forward towards the movement path of ③ (R).

⚠ In this case, ① and ② each have a long running path. They have to observe the passing behavior of the attacking players continuously and try to start the next action (handing over ④) as early as possible.

Training of offensive defense systems in youth handball
1-on-1, small groups, man coverage, and offensive defense cooperation

No. 43e	Shielding off and communicating: Pivot making a screening attempt	7	
Equipment required:	2 cones, 1 handball		

Setting:
- Define the playing field with two cones as shown in the figure.

Course:
- ① makes a step forward towards the player in ball possession.
- ④ runs forward and tries to place a screening next to ①:
  - ② moves along with ④ and forces ④ to move away from his screening position and out of the 9-meter zone (T) in order to create a 2-on-2 situation, which allows ① and ② to organize themselves and react to this new situation, according to the behavior of ① (whether he moves to the outer or to the inner side (U)).

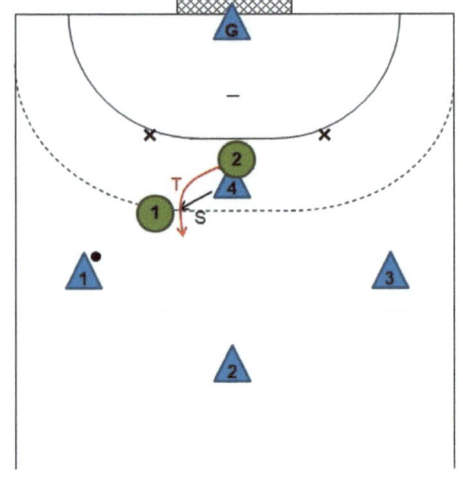
(Figure 1)

Overall course:
- The movements of ④ should be practiced in the previous exercises (43a-43e) for a sufficient length of time and on both sides alternately.

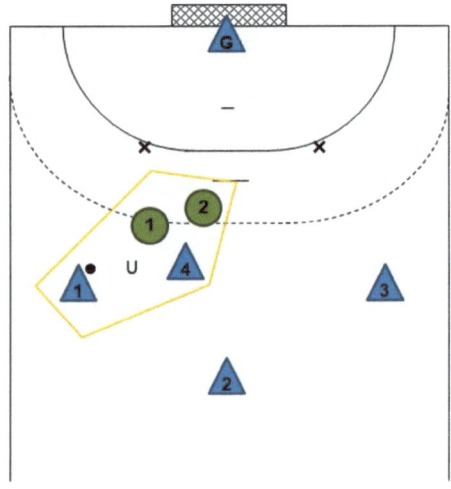
(Figure 2)

- Finally, ④ is allowed to move freely within the zone between the 6- and 9-meter lines; the two defense the two defense players should adjust their defense behavior accordingly.
- ① and ③ may also try to pass the ball to ④ directly, if ① and ② do not shield him off properly.
- If ④ has shot a goal, ① and ② must do 10 quick jumping jacks, for example.

Category: Team defense and offensive defense cooperation

1. Offensive man coverage with moving back to ball level

No. 44	Supporting each other in case of a breakthrough 3-on-3	7	★
Equipment required:	6 cones, sufficient number of handballs		

Setting:
- Define the offense corridor with cones (see figure).

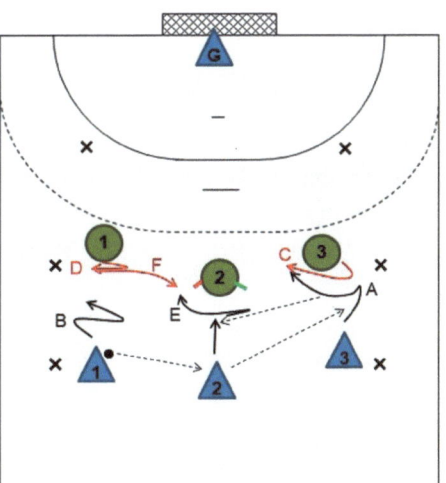

Course:
- 1, 2, and 3 play 3-on-3 against 1, 2, and 3, whereas 2 may only move in a constricted manner (he has to hold foam beams or bibs in his armpits).
- The attacking players should neither cross nor run to the 6-meter line (second pivot), but rather try to break through 1-on-1 with (B) and without (A) the ball.
- The defense players should try to prevent the players from breaking through (C and D).
- As 2 cannot move freely, primarily 2 should try to break through 1-on-1 (E).
- 1 and 3 should always observe their direct opponent but also the player in ball possession and then decide when supporting their teammates defending against a breakthrough of 2 is necessary (F).
- As soon as one of the attacking players has shot at the goal or lost the ball, the next three attacking players may start.
- Switch the defense players after several actions.

⚠ The players should time their supporting actions in such a way that they can prevent both a breakthrough and another pass.

⚠ Each player should have played defense at least once on one of the outmost defense positions.

| No. 45 | Defending and moving back to ball level | 9 | ★ |

Equipment required: 8 cones, sufficient number of handballs

Setting:
- Define a corridor with cones.

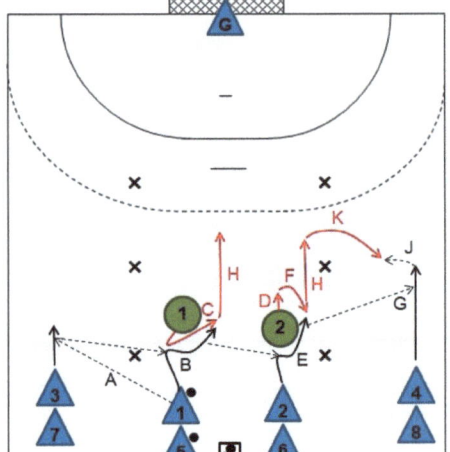

Course:
- ① and ② play 2-on-2 against ▲1 and ▲2.
- ▲3 and ▲4 are the feeders/receivers (A).
- ① and ② defend 1-on-1 against the player in ball possession (B) and try to prevent a breakthrough (C).
- While doing so, ① and ② move back to ball level (D) in order to support each other defending against any breakthrough attempts. If the direct opponent is in ball possession (E), he should be attacked 1-on-1 immediately (F).
- If one of the feeders/receivers receives a pass (G), the defense players should also move back to ball level (H).
- The feeders/receivers may pass the ball back to one of the attacking players in the corridor but also suddenly drop it (J).
- If this is the case, the defense player who is closer to the ball should leave the corridor and secure the ball as fast as he can (K).
- If an attacking player has managed to break through, he may shoot at the goal.
- As soon as the attacking players have shot at the goal or the defending players have stolen the ball, the next four attacking players may start the drill.
- In the next round, ▲3 and ▲4 become attacking players in the corridor; ▲1 and ▲2 become feeders/receivers.

⚠ Switch the defense players at regular intervals.

⚠ The defense players should always observe both the ball and their opponent to prevent a breakthrough, but also to support their teammates, and to quickly secure the ball if it was dropped.

No. 46	3-on-3 and man coverage with moving back to ball level	7	★
Equipment required:	8 cones, 1 handball		

Setting:
- Define a corridor with cones.

Course:

- ▲1, ▲2, and ▲3 play 3-on-3 against ●1, ●2, and ●3.
- While doing so, the defense players should always position themselves between their direct opponent and the goal, but move back in such a way that they can also observe the player in ball possession.
- If the direct opponent receives the ball (A), the respective defense player should attack him 1-on-1 and prevent him from breaking through (B and C).
- The other defense players move back to ball level (D and E) and support their teammate in case of a breakthrough (F).
- At the same time, they should observe their direct opponent and move along with him as soon as he starts to run without the ball. The defense player should keep his position between his opponent and the goal (H).
- As soon as an attacking player has shot at the goal, the defense players have won the ball, or the attack has been interrupted, the next attacking team may start.
- Switch the defense players after 10-15 actions.

 The players should always position themselves between their direct opponent and the goal, but move back so far that they can also observe the ball and support their teammate in case of a breakthrough.

No. 47	5-on-5 man coverage with moving back to ball level	11	★
Equipment required:	1 handball		

Course:

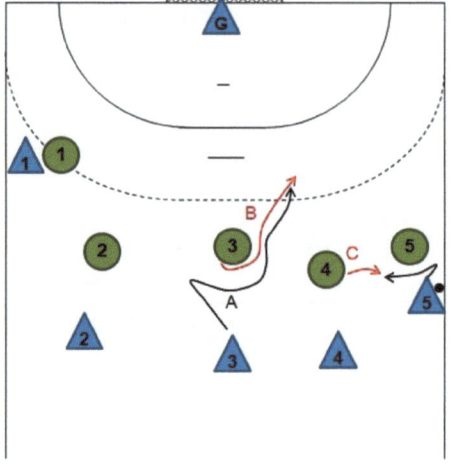

- Two teams play against each other 5-on-5.
- The defending team starts man coverage as soon as the attacking players have moved past the substitution line.
- While doing this, the defense players should move back to ball level at least so that they can observe both the ball and their opponent at the same time.
- If the respective opponent starts to run towards the goal (A), he should be followed (B).
- If a player has managed to break through with the ball, the neighboring defense players should support defending the breakthrough (C).

Overall course:

- The attacking team plays 10 attacks, then the teams switch tasks.
- The attacking players get a point for each goal. If the defense players catch and steal the ball or if the attacking players make a technical mistake, the attacking team loses a point. The teams do not get points for a miss.
- Which team has scored highest in the end?

| No. 48 | 6-on-6 man coverage with moving back to ball level | 13 | ★ |

Equipment required: 1 handball

Course:
- Two teams play against each other 6-on-6.
- The defending team plays a man coverage defense system according to the following rules:
- If a player runs towards the goal without the ball (A), the direct defending opponent should move along with him (B).
- The player in ball possession (C) should be attacked 1-on-1 (D).
- The players should always move back so far (E) that they can observe both the ball and their opponent and support their teammates in case of a breakthrough.
- ⑥ shields off the pivot to prevent passes (F).
- If an attacking player has managed to break through (G), ⑥ should support his teammate defending against the pivot (H). The other players move back (J), obstruct the passing path to the pivot, and also prevent the back position players from breaking through without the ball (K).

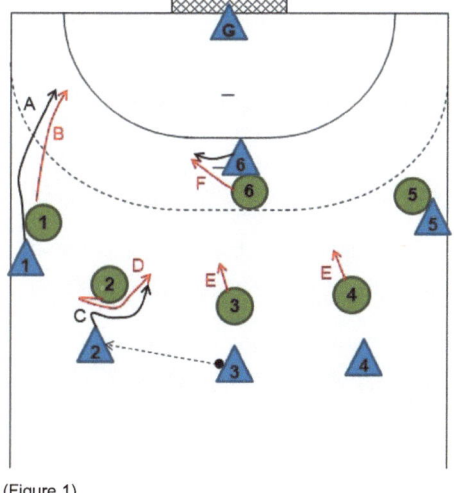
(Figure 1)

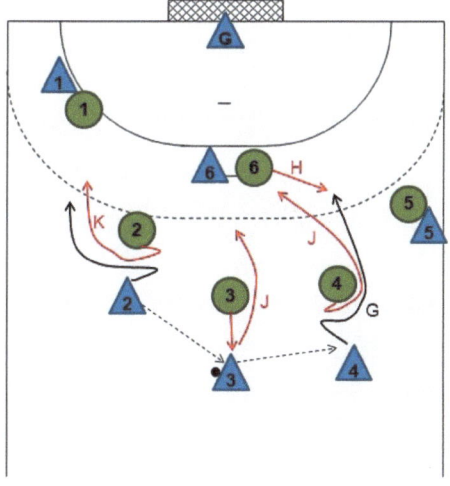
(Figure 2)

Overall course:
- The attacking team plays 10 attacks, then the teams switch tasks.
- Which defense team prevents the most goals?

2. Defending in a 1-5 defense system

No. 49	1-on-1 and defending against the pivot in a 1-5 defense system	10	★★
Equipment required:	4 cones, ball box with sufficient number of handballs		

Setting:
- Define two corridors with four cones (see figure).

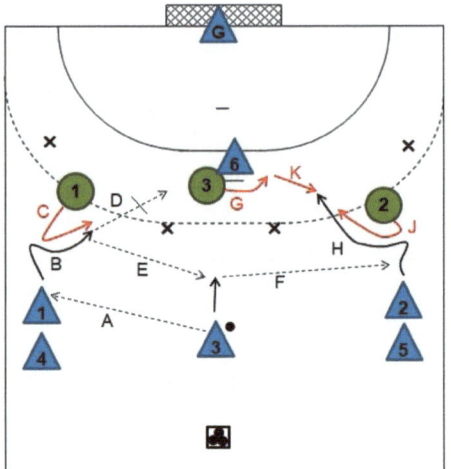

Course:
- ③ starts the drill and passes a ball to ▲1 (A).
- ▲1 tries to break through to the 6-meter line dribbling (B).
- ① actively makes a step forward towards ▲1, initiates physical contact, and tries to prevent him from breaking through (C).
- ③ shields off the pivot to prevent a pass (D).
- If ▲1 cannot break through, he passes the ball back to ③ (E), and the course starts over on the other side (F, H, and J).
- ③ runs around the pivot in order to prevent a pass again (G).
- If an attacking player has managed to break through (H), ③ supports his teammate (K) and tries to prevent the attacking player from further breaking through towards the goal zone.

⚠ ③ should recognize when he has to support his teammate defending a breakthrough, then vigorously interrupt the attacking player in a fair manner, and attack the ball in such a way, that a pass to the pivot is also almost impossible (G and K).

No. 50	1-5 defense system: Small groups of back and wing players with catching/stealing the ball on the center back position	10	★★

Equipment required: 2 foam noodles (foam beams), ball box with sufficient number of handballs

Setting:
- Define a corridor in the center with foam beams (see figure).

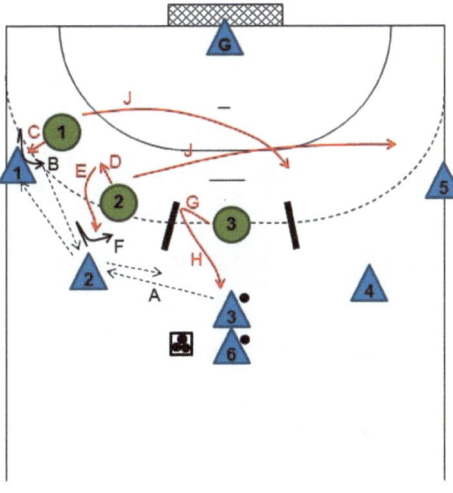

Course:
- After the initial pass from ▲3 (A), ▲1 and ▲2 play 2-on-2 against ●1 and ●2.
- ▲1 and ▲2 each try to break through to the 6-meter line 1-on-1 (B and F).
- ●1 and ●2 actively make a step forward towards their opponent 1-on-1 (C and E). As soon as their direct opponent is no longer in ball possession, they move back a bit (D) in order to be able to support their teammates.
- If ▲2 receives the ball, ●3 should move back a bit to get in a supporting position (G).
- As soon as ▲2 dribbles or holds the ball, i.e. apparently cannot break through, ●3 makes a step forward and obstructs the passing path to ▲3 (H).
- Afterwards, ●1 and ●2 run to the other side (J), and the course starts over with ●6, ●4, and ●5.

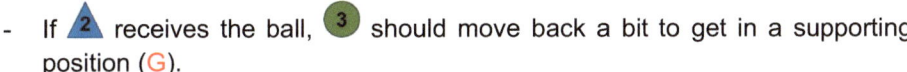 ●1 and ●2 should actively attack their opponent and prevent him from breaking through and/or steal the ball when the attacking player is dribbling it. If the attacking players keep passing the ball, the defense players move back a bit in order to be able to support their teammates.

⚠ ●3 should recognize when ▲2 has finished his action and then interrupt or block the pass to the center back (H).

No. 51a	1-5 defense system 4-on-4	9	★★
Equipment required:	2 cones, ball box with sufficient number of handballs		

Setting:
- Define the playing field with two cones.

Course:

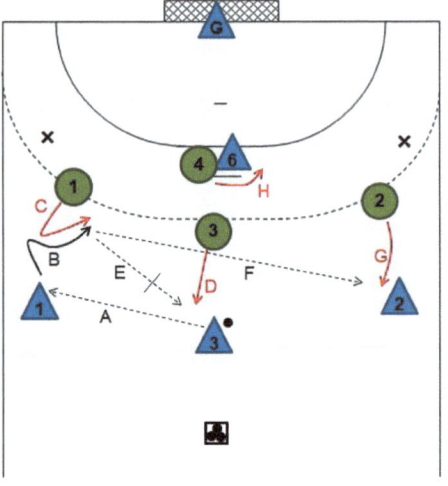

- 3 starts the drill and passes a ball to 1 (A).
- 1 tries to break through to the 6-meter line dribbling (B).
- 1 actively makes a step forward towards 1, initiates physical contact, and prevents him from breaking through (C).
- 4 shields off the pivot to prevent a pass and secures the zone to prevent any breakthroughs.

(Figure 1)

- As soon as 1 interrupts his breakthrough attempt, 3 offensively makes a step forward towards 3 (D) to prevent a pass (E).
- If 1 plays a long pass to 2 (F), 2 tries to interrupt the pass and to catch and steal the ball (G).
- 4 runs around the pivot (H) and secures the zone to prevent a pass.

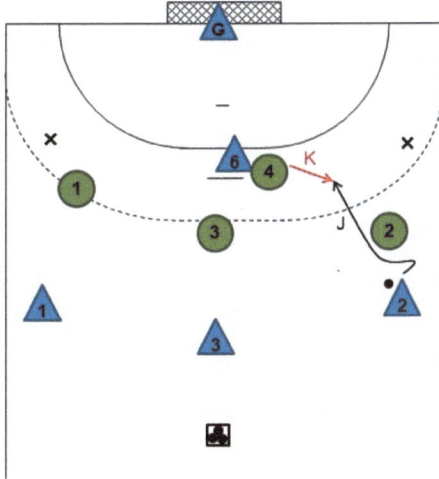
(Figure 2)

- If ② cannot catch and steal the ball, he should attack ② and prevent him from breaking through.
- If an attacking player has managed to break through (J), ④ should support his teammate (K) by trying to prevent him from further breaking through towards the goal zone and by attacking the ball in such a way that a pass to the pivot is also almost impossible.
- As soon as the attack is over or the defense players have won the ball, the next four attacking players may start an attack.
- Change the defense players after several actions.

⚠ The defense players should carefully observe the attacking players' next steps and immediately react in a highly dynamic manner.

No. 51b	1-5 defense system 6-on-6	13	★★
Equipment required:	Ball box with sufficient number of handballs		

Course:

- The players play a free 6-on-6 game.
- The defending team plays an offensive 1-5 defense system.
- If their direct opponent is in ball possession, the respective defense players ②, ③, and ④ should initiate physical contact and prevent a breakthrough (A).
- If a back player interrupts his breakthrough attempt, the neighboring defense player should make a step forward (B) to force a long pass.
- The defense players may attack long passes immediately (C).
- The defense player on the center back position (⑥) shields off the pivot in such a way that he cannot receive a pass (D).
- If a back player has managed to break through, ⑥ should support his teammate (E) and try to prevent him from breaking through further towards the goal zone and also try to prevent a pass to the pivot.
- The attacking team plays 10 attacks, then the teams switch tasks. Which defense team prevents the most goals?

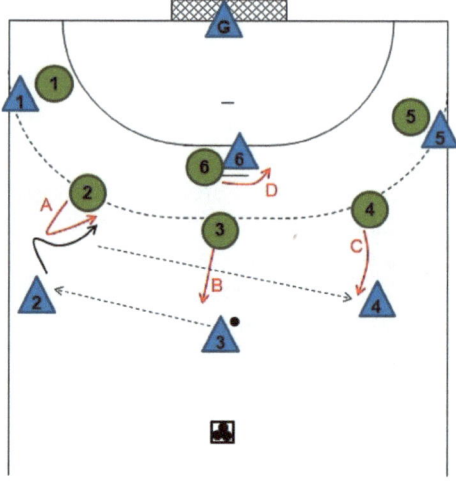

(Figure 1)

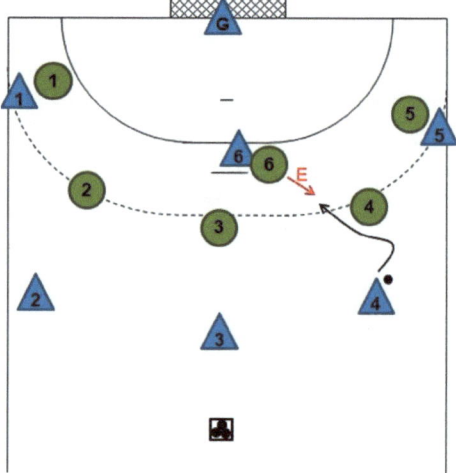

(Figure 2)

Variant:

- In the beginning, the back players are not allowed to change positions.
- Allow positional changes in the second round, if applicable.
- Each defense player should defend the zone within his corridor.
- In case of positional changes right in front of the defense line, the attacking players should be handed over, whereas a second pivot should be followed.

No. 52a	Defending against a second pivot from the wing position	12	★★

Equipment required: 2 cones, ball box with sufficient number of handballs

Setting:
- Define the shooting zone with cones.

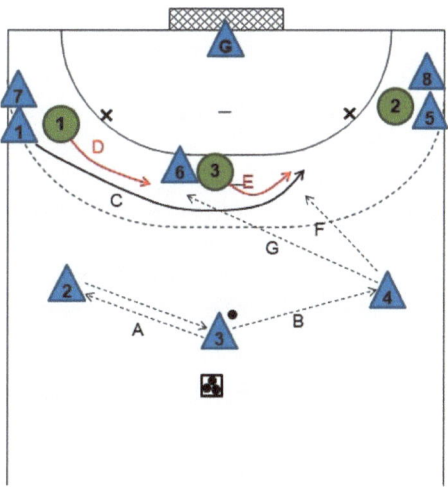

Course:
- The players on the back positions, ②, ③, and ④, keep passing the ball (A and B).
- Anytime during the passing, ① leaves his position and becomes the second pivot (C).
- ① moves along with ①, so that he cannot receive a pass (D) and – depending on the running path of ① and the position of ⑥ at the 6-meter line – must communicate with ③ to clarify who is in charge of the second and first pivot (E).
- The back players try to pass the ball to the second pivot (F) or first pivot (G).
- Following a pass (attempt), ③ picks up a new ball from the ball box, and the course starts over with ⑤ becoming the second pivot and ② defending against him.
- ① and ① line up on the other side and switch tasks (defense/offense).

⚠ The defending wing players should move along with the players running towards the 6-meter line and initiate physical contact in order to prevent them from getting to the 6-meter line uninterruptedly.

⚠ Following the positional change, the defense players should communicate and clarify who is in charge of the second and first pivot.

No. 52b	Defending against a second pivot from the back position by moving along and handing over	9	★★
Equipment required:	2 cones, ball box with sufficient number of handballs		

Setting:
- Define the playing field with two cones.

Course:
- The players play 4-on-4.
- The attacking team's instruction is to run to the 6-meter line (second pivot) without the ball; they may also try to break through 1-on-1, however.
- Each attacking player should initially cover his corridor and defend (B) 1-on-1 breakthrough attempts (A) of the respective attacking player.
- If an attacking player has managed to get to the 6-meter line (C), the respective defense player should move along with him (D).
- The other defense players of the foremost defense line (1 and 3) should keep defending against the respective opponents (F) and try to prevent them from breaking through.
- The two defense players at the 6-meter line (2 and 4) try to prevent passes to the pivot, communicate with each other in case of positional changes (G and H), and hand/take over (J) accordingly.
- In addition, 2 and 4 should support their teammates defending against any breakthroughs (not shown in the figure).

(Figure 1)

(Figure 2)

⚠ Switch the defense players at regular intervals.

No. 52c	1-5 defense system 6-on-6	13	★★
Equipment required:	Ball box with sufficient number of handballs		

Course:
- The players play a free 6-on-6 game.
- The defending team plays an offensive 1-5 defense system.
- If their direct opponent is in ball possession, the defense players of the foremost defense line (2, 3, and 4) should initiate physical contact and prevent a breakthrough 1-on-1 (A and B).
- If two attacking players cross (with or without the ball) in front of the defense line (C), the defense players should communicate with each other and hand/take over the attacking players accordingly (D and E).
- If a wing player becomes the second pivot (F), his opponent must run along with him towards the 6-meter line (G).
- A back player becoming the second pivot (H) should also be followed by his opponent towards the 6-meter line (J).
- Following the positional change (second pivot), the defense players at the 6-meter line should communicate with each other and hand/take over the pivots accordingly.

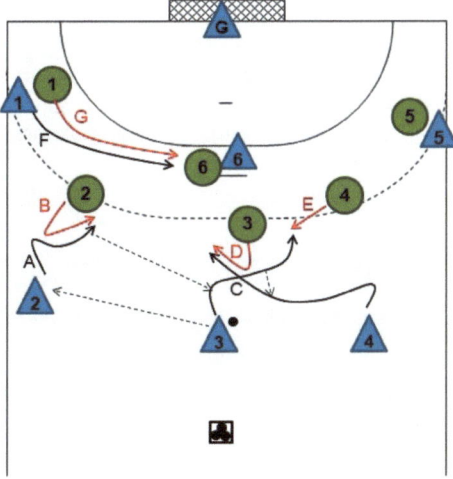
(Figure 1)

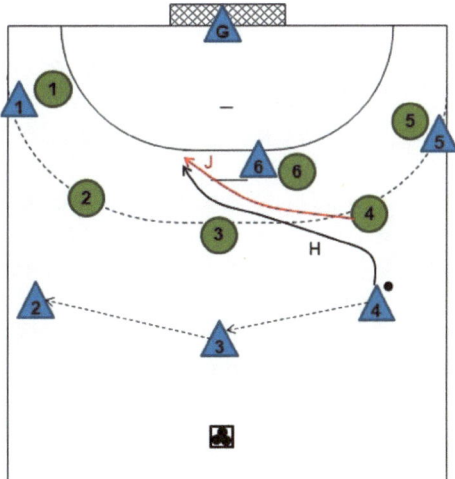
(Figure 2)

Overall course:
- The attacking team plays 10 attacks.
  If the attacking players shoot a goal, they get a point; if the defense team directly wins the ball (catching and stealing it), the attacking team loses a point; in case of a miss or technical error, no points are awarded.
- Switch the tasks after 10 attacks.
- Which team has scored highest in the end?

3. Defending in a 3-3 defense system

No. 53	3-on-3 defense in a corridor against positional changes of the attacking players	10	★★
Equipment required:	4 cones, ball box with sufficient number of handballs		

Setting:
- Define the playing field with cones (see figure).

Course:
- ▲1, ▲2, and ▲3 play 3-on-3 against three defense players, ●1, ●2, and ●3.
- ●1, ●2, and ●3 stand offensively, in front of the 9-meter line.
- The attacking players should try to outnumber the defense players through positional changes:
  o Either by crossing of a player behind the player in ball possession (C and D), immediately after the initial passes (A and B) (see figure 1).
  o Or by initiating a positional change of two players (H), with the third player holding the ball (G) (see figure 2).
- The defense players should communicate and hand/take over (E and F, or J and K) the attacking players accordingly.
- As soon as an attacking player has shot at the goal or lost the ball, the next group of 3 may start an attack.

Overall course:
- The defending team of 3 must play against each attacking team five times; the teams switch tasks afterwards.
- Which attacking team has scored the most goals?

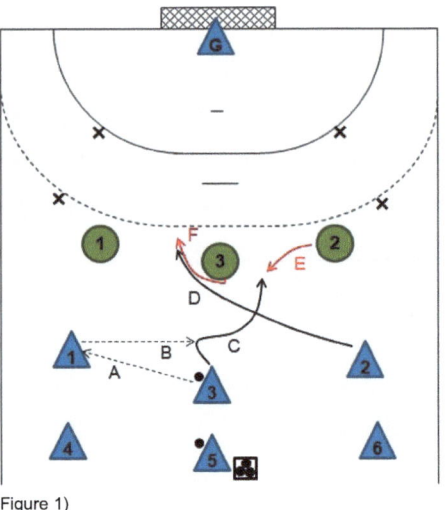
(Figure 1)

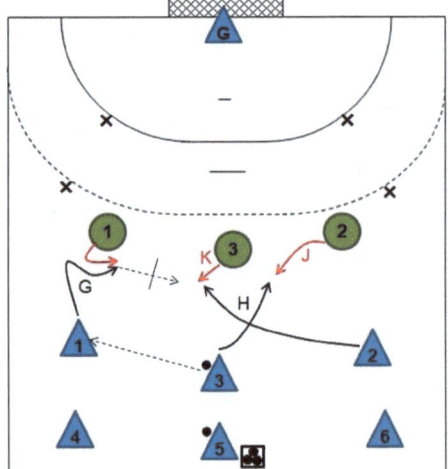
(Figure 2)

⚠ The defense players should communicate and coordinate the handing/taking over and quickly move to the respective attacking player.

⚠ In order to do the handing/taking over properly, the defense players must move back to ball level already when covering their respective opponent.

No. 54	3-3 defense system: Foremost defense line against crossing moves and second pivot	10	★★
Equipment required:	4 cones, ball box with sufficient number of handballs		

Setting:
- Define a broad corridor for the back players with cones.

Course:
- ①, ②, and ③ play defense against ▲1, ▲2, and ▲3.
- The attacking players may play a free game and try to outnumber the defense players through passes (A), 1-on-1 actions, crossings (B), and playing with a second pivot (C).
- The defense players should move along with the second pivot, even if he is about to overlap the other defense players (D); they also should always try to position themselves between the goal and their respective opponent in order to prevent any breakthrough attempts.
- If the attacking players cross (B), the defense players should communicate quickly and hand/take over their opponents (E).

⚠ When attacking players are handed/taken over, the defense players should communicate this with each other loudly.

⚠ Switch the defense players at regular intervals.

No. 55	3-3 defense system: Defending on the wing and center back positions	11	★★
Equipment required:	Ball box with sufficient number of handballs		

Course (figure 1):

- ①, ②, and ③ play defense against ▲1, ▲5, and ▲6.
- ▲2, ▲3, and ▲4 provide the balls as feeders/receivers.
- By passing the ball back and forth on the back positions (A and B), the attacking players try to either pass the ball to one of the wing players in such a way that he can approach the goal (E and G), or to pass the ball to ▲6 (K) who is trying to get in a good position for a pass near the 6-meter line (J).

(Figure 1)

- ① and ③ try to force the wing players to shoot from an unfavorable position by pushing them further aside as soon as they have received the ball (F).
- The attacking wing players may shoot (G) or pass the ball back to one of the back players (H).
- As soon as the ball is on the opposite side, the defending wing players move towards the inner side a bit (D).
- ② shields off the pivot in such a way that he cannot receive a pass (K). He should always try to position himself between the player in ball possession and the pivot (C) and to immediately react to the pivot's movements by maintaining physical contact (L).
- As soon as one of the attacking players has shot at the goal, they each move on to the next position on the right; the right wing player moves to the left wing position, the left wing player lines up for the left back position with a ball.

Extended course (figure 2):

- The course remains the same as shown in figure 1.
- In addition, the attacking wing players now may act as a second pivot (M) and try to get in a good position for a pass (P).
- The defending wing player moves along with the second pivot (N) and tries to prevent a pass, if possible.

(Figure 2)

⚠ The defending wing player initially moves along with the second pivot. Depending on the running path of the first pivot, he might communicate with ② to organize the handing/taking over.

⚠ Switch the defense players at regular intervals.

No. 56	3-3 defense system 6-on-6	13	★★
Equipment required:	1 handball		

Course:
- Finally, the exercises no. 53, 54, and 55 are combined.
- The attacking team tries to score a goal against the 3-3 defending team.
- The defense players try to implement the running paths and instructions from the three previous exercises and to prevent goals.
- Switch tasks after several attacks.

Defense tasks:
- The defending wing players try to force the attacking wing players to shoot from an unfavorable position by obstructing the way to the inner side and pushing the attacking wing player further aside.
- As soon as the ball is on the opposite side, the defending wing players move towards the inner side a bit in order to narrow the gaps. While doing so, they always have to watch out for a second pivot and move along with them, if necessary.
- The center defense player on the 6-meter line covers the pivot and shields him off so that he cannot receive a pass. He should maintain physical contact to be able to immediately react to the pivot's movements.
- The players defending against the attacking back players should always position themselves between the goal and their direct opponent.

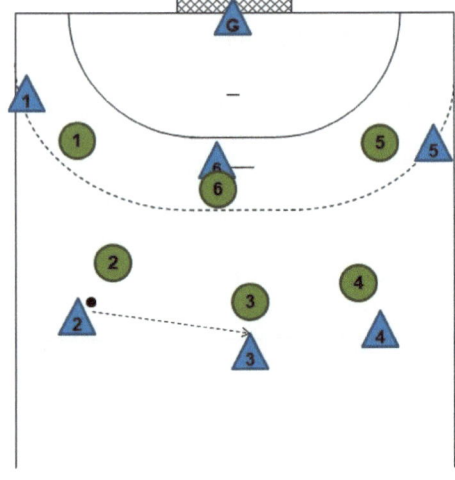

(Figure 1)

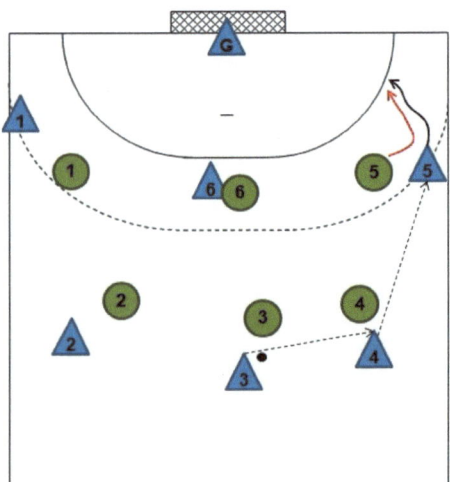

(Figure 2)

4. Defending in a 3-2-1 defense system

The 3-2-1 defense system is the first transitional step to more defensive defense systems. The defense players no longer align with the opposing attacking player's position, but rather move in a ball-oriented manner for the first time. However, what should be kept in mind is that moving closer to the side where the ball is being passed may offer some advantages, but there will always be an outnumbered defense on the opposite side. This brings about new challenges for the defense players. They do not only have to stick to certain rules of movement but also focus on communicating with each other. Crossing movements in front of the defense line and the second pivot movements behind the defense line must be communicated properly. The attacking players are no longer followed in any case, but rather handed over to the next defense player.

No. 57	Preparatory 1-on-1 exercise and moving back to the pivot	10	★★★
Equipment required:	4 poles, ball box with sufficient number of handballs		

Setting:
- Define the playing corridors with four poles as shown in the figure.

Course:
- ▲1, ▲2, and ▲6 play 3-on-3 against ●1, ●2, and ●3; ●5 is the feeder/receiver.
- As soon as ●5 passes to ▲1 (A), ▲1 makes a step forward and tries to interrupt (C) a possible 1-on-1 action (B) of ●1.
- ▲3 moves along and supports his teammate (D), if ●1 tries to break through; ▲2 prevents a pass to ▲6 at the 6-meter line.
- If the players pass the ball to ●5 (E) and to the other side, to ▲2 (F), ●2 makes a step forward towards ▲2 (G), ▲3 moves behind ●2 (H) and hence closes the gap, and ▲1 moves back to the 6-meter line again in order to cover the pivot.
- Change the defense players after several actions.

⚠ The defense players should actively step forward towards the player in ball possession.

⚠ Following the defense action, the defense players should reorient immediately and move to the side where the ball is being passed.

No. 58	4-on-4 defense diamond	8	★★★
Equipment required:	2 poles, ball box with sufficient number of handballs		

Setting:
- Define the playing field with two poles.

Course:
- 🔺1, 🔺2, 🔺3, and 🔺6 play 4-on-4 against 🔵1, 🔵2, 🔵3, and 🔵4.
- As soon as 🔺3 passes the ball to 🔺1 (A), 🔵1 makes a clear step forward and tries to interrupt (C) a possible 1-on-1 action (B) of 🔺1.
- 🔵3 moves along and supports his teammate (D), if 🔺1 tries to

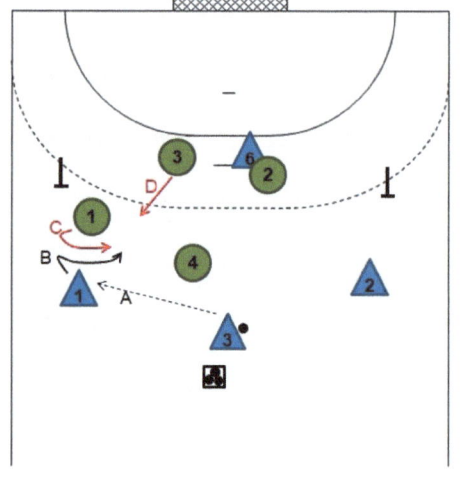

(Figure 1)

break through; 🔵2 prevents a pass to 🔺6 at the 6-meter line, and 🔵4 also slightly moves along to the side where the ball is being passed.

- If the ball is passed back to 🔺3 (E), 🔵4 makes a clear step forward towards 🔺3 (F).
- As soon as 🔺3 passes to 🔺2 (G), 🔵2 steps forward towards 🔺2 (H), 🔵3 moves to the side where the ball is being passed and hence closes the gap behind 🔵2 (J). 🔵1 moves back to the 6-meter line (K) and helps defending against 🔺6, who is moving along the 6-meter line, whereas 🔵4 closes the gap in direction where the ball is being passed (L).

(Figure 2)

- The attacking team plays 10 attacks, then the teams switch tasks. In the first round, the players should avoid crossing and running along the 6-meter line (second pivot); allow crossing and running along the 6-meter line (second pivot) in the further course of the drill.

⚠ The defense players should actively step forward towards the player in ball possession.

⚠ Following the defense action, the defense players should reorient immediately and move to the side where the ball is being passed.

No. 59	Offensive defense wing player on the opposite side in a 3-2-1 defense system	8	★★★
Equipment required:	2 cones, ball box with sufficient number of handballs		

Setting:
- Position two cones in line with the goal posts.

Course 1:
- ① and ② practice the running moves of the defending wing players in a 3-2-1 defense system with offensive wing players on the opposite side; ③ acts as the defense player on the center front position.
- The players pass the ball several times from left to right (A to E) and from right to left (figure 1).
- During the pass from the center to the right back (D), the defense wing player who is on the opposite side of the player in ball possession (①) steps forward offensively (F).
- As soon as the players pass the ball back to the center and to the other side again, the defense wing players move back again to their initial defense wing position (C).

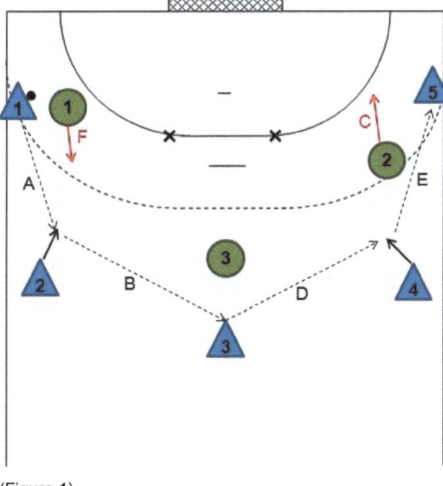

(Figure 1)

Course 2:

- Extension of the basic move: The players may play a long pass from back position to back position.
- During the pass from the attacking wing player to the back player (G), ③ steps forward into the passing path to ③ (H) and hence forces a long pass from ④ to ② (J).
- ① tries to catch the long pass from the offensive position he took over before (K). ① must not start too soon, as otherwise ④ could possibly play a pass to ① (L).

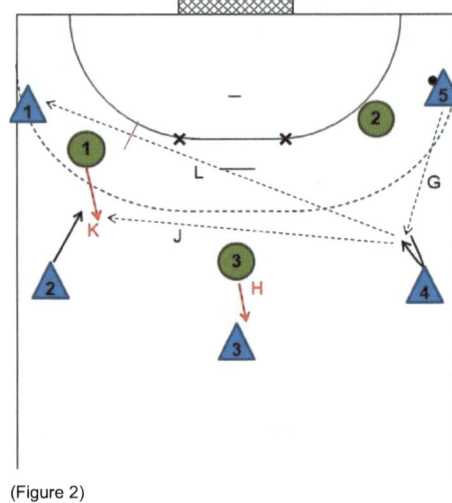

(Figure 2)

- Switch tasks after several ball stealing and catching attempts of both defense wing players.

⚠ The back position players should start to run towards the passing path as they would do in a real game, even though they know that the wing player could try to catch the ball.

⚠ The wing players should try to catch the ball as close to their opponent as possible.

No. 60	3-2-1 defense system 6-on-6	13	★★★
Equipment required:	1 handball		

Course 1:

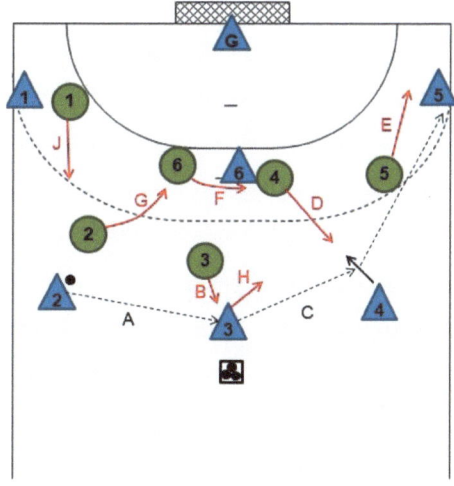

- Two teams play against each other 6-on-6.
- The defending team plays a 3-2-1 defense system.
- As soon as ② passes the ball to ③ (A), ③ vigorously steps forward towards ③ (B).
- As soon as ③ passes the ball to ④ (C), ④ steps forward towards ④ (D), and ⑤ moves back to his initial wing position (E).
- ⑥ closes the gap behind ④ (F) and takes over ⑥.
- ② moves back to the 6-meter line (G) and supports his teammate defending against the pivot (⑥), ③ moves towards the side where the ball is being passed (H).
- ① steps forward offensively (J) in order to prevent a long pass from ④ to ②.
- The attacking players initially pass the ball back and forth several times, the defense players initially move as usual, according to the 3-2-1 defense system.
- Afterwards, the attacking team may play five attacks, without crossing movements and without a second pivot, however.
- The players switch tasks after five attacks
- Which team has shot the most goals?

Course 2:
- The attacking team may now also add crossing movements; the defense players should communicate with each other in case of positional changes of the attacking players.

Editor's note

In 1995, a friend convinced me to join him in coaching a handball youth team (male, under 13 years of age).

This was the beginning of my career as a team handball coach. Ever since I enjoyed working as a coach and had high requirements concerning my exercises. Soon, the standard pool of exercises wasn't enough for me anymore and I started to modify and develop drills myself.

Today, I coach a broad range of youth and adult teams with different performance levels and adjust my training units to the individual needs of the teams.

A few years ago, I started selling my exercises and drills online at handball-uebungen.de. Since, in handball training, there is a tendency towards a general athletic training that focuses on coordination work – especially in the training of youth teams –, a large number of my games and exercises can be applied to other sports as well.

Get inspired by the various game concepts, be creative, and rely on your own experiences!

Milestones of my career as a coach
- As of July 2012: A-License, DHB
- As of November 2011: Editor (handball-uebungen.de, Handball Practice, and Special Handball Practice)
- 2008-2010: Youth coordinator and youth coach, SG Leutershausen (Germany)
- Since 2006: B-License

Yours sincerely,
Jörg Madinger

Further reference books published by DV Concept

From warm-up to handball team play – 75 exercises for every handball training unit

By making your training units more diverse, you can increase the players' motivation, since you consistently offer new approaches to improve and refine familiar movement sequences. In this book, you will find inspiring exercises you can apply during each phase of your everyday team handball training – from warm-up and goalkeeper warm-up shooting to the common contents of the main phase and the closing games. Each exercise is illustrated and described in an easy, comprehensible manner. Specific notes give you tips on what you need to be aware of.

This book deals with the following key subjects:

Warm-up:
- Basic warm-up
- Short warm-up games
- Sprint contests
- Coordination
- Ball familiarization
- Goalkeeper warm-up shooting

Basic exercises, basic play, and target play:
- Offense/series of shots
- General offense
- Fast throw-off
- 1st and 2nd wave
- Defensive action
- Closing games
- Endurance

At the end of this book, you will find an entire methodological training unit. The objective of this training unit is to improve shooting and quick decision-making under pressure.

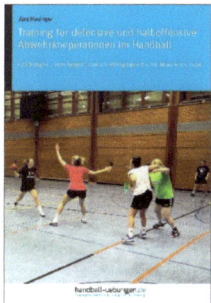

Training of defensive and semi-offensive cooperative defense strategies for handball teams

60 exercises – From 1-on-1 to small group and team defense

A good defense is a prerequisite for modern team handball. The intention is not only to prevent goals but also to actively win the ball and subsequently initiate a fast attack. The offense should permanently be put under pressure and forced to make mistakes.

The exercises in this collection initially deal with the individual basics of defense play. Individual and position-specific training marks the starting point for subsequent cooperative defense play and allows for choosing the appropriate defense system. The basics both include exercises on legwork, 1-on-1 defense and covering the pivot in combination with fast adjustment to subsequent actions as well as blocking and anticipating on the wing positions of a proactive defense system.

The second part of the collection deals with cooperative small group defense play and focuses on handing over/taking over attacking players along the defense line (width of defense) and on making agreements when defending against the pivot.

The third chapter introduces cooperative team defense in 6-0, 5-1, 3-2-1, and 4-2 defense systems along with possible variants.

Get inspired by the exercises, develop your own defense concepts, and make use of the individual strengths of your defense players for optimal cooperation.

Passing and catching while moving – 60 exercises for each handball training unit

Passing and catching are two basic handball techniques which must be trained and improved continuously. These 60 practical exercises offer you various options to train passing and catching in a challenging and diverse manner. The exercises particularly focus on improving passing and catching skills even during highly dynamic movements. The drills therefore combine new running paths and movements similar to real game situations.

Effective goalkeeper warm-up shooting – 60 exercises for every handball unit

Goalkeeper warm-up shooting is essential for almost every training unit. These 60 warm-up shooting exercises provide you with a variety of ideas to make the warm-up shooting challenging and diverse, both for the goalkeepers and the field players. The exercises particularly focus on improving the players' dynamics even during the warm-up shooting.

Coordinative handball training with different equipment
6 diverse training units with 44 single exercises

Six training units deal with six different handball-specific topics. The training units focus on small-sized equipment that is available in the gym or common toys (dice or game of cards). In combination with the common gym equipment, handball-specific content is delivered in new challenging ways which allows you to organize your training units in a new and diverse fashion over and over again. Whether playing with a game of cards, a dice, balloons, bibs, small gym mats, or hoops – the collection of drills shows you the great versatility of each item. The training units should encourage you to be creative, develop your own ideas, and give you examples of how simple resources can help you to deliver recurring content in new ways over and over again and to make sure that your training units are fun.

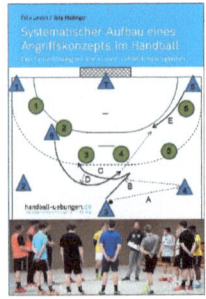

Systematic development of handball offense concepts – Game opening with variants and continuous playing options

Based on crossing of the center back and the pivot (circle) – which is part of almost every team's repertoire in various forms – Felix Linden explains how you can create different game situations by using simple extensions and hence overcome defense systems with many variants. The individual training units deal with essential elements such as pulling apart a 6-0 defense system, authentic piston movements, pulling out a defense player, different shooting options, and decision-making. All training units focus on decision-making processes in particular. The training units comprise the standard playing structures with continuous playing options on both sides, variants with a second pivot and position switching as well as a variant for game situations with numerical superiority.

Competitive games for your everyday handball training – 60 exercises for each age-group

Handball needs quick and correct decisions in each game situation. This can be trained playfully and diversely through handball-specific games. These 60 exercises are divided into seven categories and train the playing skills.

The book deals with the following subjects:
- Team ball variants
- Team play with different targets
- Tag games
- Sprint and relay race games
- Ball throwing and transportation games
- Games from other types of sports
- Complex closing game variants

Minihandball training and handball training for young kids (5 training units)

Minihandball training and handball training for kids is different from handball training for older players and considerably different from handball training for competitive players. During their first contact with "handball", kids should be familiarized with the ball in a playful way. They should be taught that being active, doing sports, playing together, and even playing against each other is fun.

This book contains a short introduction to handball for kids and young children and its special characteristics as well as example exercises which help to make your training units interesting and more diverse.

Following this, there are five complete training units of different difficulty levels that focus on the basic handball techniques (dribbling, passing, catching, shooting, and defending in a game with opponents). The kids are playfully introduced to the subsequent handball-specific basics. At the same time, particular attention is payed to general physical experience and the development of coordination skills.

The exercises are illustrated and described in an easy, comprehensible manner. They can be immediately integrated in every training unit. By using the given training variants, you can easily adjust the difficulty level of the training units to the respective target group. The variants should also encourage you to modify and further develop the exercises to make each training unit a new and more diverse experience for the children.

Paperback from the Handball Practice series (Handball Praxis) (five training units each)

Handball Practice 9 – Basic training for youth teams of 9-12 years of age

Handball Practice 10 – Modern speed handball: Fast adjustment to the 1st and 2nd wave

Handball Practice 14 – Interaction of back position players with the pivot – Shifting, Screening, and Using the Russian Screen

Special Handball Practice 1 – Step-by-step training of a 3-2-1 defense system (6 training units)

Special Handball Practice 2 – Step-by-step training for successful offense strategies against the 6-0 defense system (6 training units)

For further reference and e-books visit us at:
www.en.handball-uebungen.de

www.ingramcontent.com/pod-product-compliance
Lightning Source LLC
Chambersburg PA
CBHW041803160426
43191CB00001B/18